Seven eLements of Leadership for a New Breed of Leader

Michael A. Pitcher

Seven eLements of Leadership for a New Breed of Leader

Copyright © 2016 Michael A. Pitcher

All Rights Reserved. Published 2016.

No part of this publication may be reproduced, distributed, or transmitted in any form or by any means, including photocopying, recording, or other electronic or mechanical methods, without the prior written permission of the publisher, ex-cept in the case of brief quotations embodied in critical reviews and certain other noncommercial uses permitted by copyright law. For permission requests, write to the publisher, addressed   Attention: Permissions Coordinator,   at the address below.

ISBN: 978-0-9971689-0-7

Library of Congress Control Number: 2015921307

Printed in the United States of America

Michael A. Pitcher
P.O. Box 368
Alpharetta, GA 30009-0368
www.MikePitcher.net

To the women in my life:
My wife, Sheri, and daughters, Lauren, Michelle,
Mckensie, and Morgan.
I love you all more than you know.

Acknowledgments

This book wouldn't be possible without my family. First, to my wife, Sheri: I am eternally grateful for your patience, your guidance, your friendship, and your unconditional love. You make me a better man. I have heard it said that one should not have to change anything for the person one marries, but I'm not sure this is a true statement, as every day I want to be a better man for you. And as far as that whole soul mate thing goes, we've got this! I love you.

To our amazing children: Lauren, Michelle, Mckensie, and Morgan. Each of you are so incredibly different, each with a unique set of gifts and talents. I have been blessed to watch you grow and mature from children to adolescents, and now to young adults. I could not be more proud of you, and I cannot wait to see what the future holds for each of you.

Sincere thanks to my mother, Gloria, my father, Bob, and my two brothers, Danny and Robbie, for a rock-solid foundation. You continually impressed on me the importance of a good education and hard work.

Speaking of hard work, my business career has placed me in the presence of some incredible people who have had a great influence on my life. During my twenty years with Pitney Bowes, I was blessed with the opportunity to work with and learn from dozens of exceptional leaders, including Mike O'Connell, Sonny Campbell, Mike Quigley, Jerry Graham, Mary Maarbjerg, Mary Fahey, Mark Misiti, and Rick Butzek. Thanks to Mike Critelli, CEO of Pitney Bowes, for providing me with several valuable learning experiences.

While at Dell and Dell Financial Services, I was privileged to work with CEO Michael Watt, DJ DiMarco, one of the most colorful experts in the leasing game, and a "young gun" named Darren Fedorowicz. Each of them impacted the leader I would become.

During the last eleven years with LeasePlan, it has been my distinct pleasure to work side by side with some of the most dedicated professionals I have ever been associated with. From the international side of our business, Vahid Daemi and Kevin McNally have provided guidance and direction on a regular basis. Within LeasePlan USA, I've had the good fortune of being part of an incredibly talented leadership team. The members of this team include Dave Dahm, John Jaje, Jon Toups, Mary Christy, Paul Kennedy, Nancy Damico, and Tim Martin. This team provides me the opportunity to learn something new every day.

While the previously mentioned individuals are all associated with my business career, I'd also like to acknowledge and thank a few teachers and professors and a dear friend. As a freshman in high school, I met and became friends with the principal of Chalmette High School, Mr. Wayne Warner. He is still in this role today, living the lesson he taught me: A good education is a critical element of success, but only when paired with a great work ethic. During my pursuit of an MBA at Emory University, I had the good fortune of meeting Rick Gilkey, a professor of organizational behavior, who understands that complex business organizations are built on human relationships. I had the privilege and pleasure of working for more than thirty years with the executive director of Theta Xi Fraternity, Jim Vredenburg. Unfortunately, Jim lost a battle with cancer in 2013. We enjoyed so many conversations about being a leader. Early in my career, he advised me that "true leadership is a one-on-one experience." I have never forgotten that advice.

I'd also like to thank my team of beta readers for providing valuable input and feedback for improving the content of this book. I want you to know that your suggestions and recommendations are truly appreciated. This team included Stuart Altemeyer, Sara Bell,

Acknowledgments

Kevin Giddins, Tom Grace, Annick Schoon, and Ryan Roberts. And Annick, my Dutch friend, thanks for the global perspective.

Lastly, I would like to acknowledge my writing coach, Anita Henderson. Anita is called "The Author's Midwife," and she helps struggling authors take a dream and make it reality. I am confident that I was one of her most difficult assignments. Anita pushed and prodded, challenged and cajoled, but if you are reading this book, she accomplished her objective. Anita, I would like to thank you for staying the course with this very difficult pupil.

Contents

Foreword 1
Introduction 3
Chapter 1: LAUGH 11
Chapter 2: LEARN 29
Chapter 3: LISTEN 51
Chapter 4: LANGUAGE 65
Chapter 5: LAGNIAPPE 89
Chapter 6: LEGACY 107
Chapter 7: LOVE 123
Epilogue: My Wish 143
About the Author 149
Suggested Reading for Leaders 151

Foreword

Mike Pitcher represents the best of a new generation of leaders who understand that leadership is the ability to create an environment where everyone can achieve their potential. This leadership style is ultimately the secret sauce that develops the talent to implement with heartfelt purpose and passion. His recognized track record for leading companies that consistently win "Best Places to Work" awards attests to his passion and commitment for building corporate cultures that inspire, engage, and perform.

As this book demonstrates, Mike's energy, humor, and authenticity (yes, he is a real product of Louisiana's Cajun culture) are all beautifully expressed through his Seven eLements of Leadership. While there are many books espousing leadership principles, Mike has attained noteworthy success, not just because he teaches these principles well, but because he lives them, every single day, and he inspires others to do the same.

The Seven eLements of Leadership are well-illustrated with charming, real stories of Mike's own odyssey as a leader. He gives specific suggestions so the reader can easily assimilate the key lessons and apply them. The remarkable feature of Mike's stories is that (just as in real life) he tells of his failure and mistakes with as much passion and energy as his success stories. I think this is because Mike knows that leadership is not a game for the fainthearted or risk averse.

Leaders often learn more from their failures than from their successes. While Mike is an example of this intuitive leadership style, there is also a serious body of research that supports his views and practices. In one of the most noteworthy pieces of longitudinal leadership research conducted by the Center for Creative Leadership, a key finding was that successful leaders all suffer from setbacks and failures. Therefore, leadership success is not the absence of failure; it is the ability to deal with it. In the long run, authenticity ("Yes, I've made mistakes") and resilience ("and I know how to recover from them") carry the day in leadership. As a leader and as an author, Mike helps everyone become more successful. I daresay reading this book can make you a better person. Who doesn't need to listen better and laugh more?

Finally, Mike's leadership stories will delight you, amuse you, and inspire you to be a better leader no matter how experienced you are, or are not, at this moment. This is what I call Mike's magic—he makes everyone better for having been in his company. I hope you enjoy this book as much as all of us who have been a part of Mike's wonderful journey have enjoyed being a part of it.

Roderick Gilkey, PhD
Professor in the Practice of Organization & Management
Goizueta Business School, Emory University
Professor of Psychiatry and Behavioral Sciences
Emory University School of Medicine

Introduction

In 2003, I interviewed with my friend—although not a friend at that time—Dave Dahm for a C-level role with LeasePlan USA. I explained to Dave that I was working on a book about leadership, to be titled The Seven eLements. As I sit down today to work on this introduction, I am no closer to that objective than these three sentences.

Perhaps the trigger of being more than a half-century old, the emotional pain of a divorce after a twenty-year marriage, the joy in a new marriage, or tears shed while walking two of my four daughters down the aisle, has brought me to this place. The fear of failure, or the thought that no one would be interested in what I had to say about leadership, prevented me from putting pen to paper (or fingers to a keyboard). Now, I've reached a point in my life that if the only readers of this book are my four daughters, then I will consider this adventure a success.

Earlier in my career, I went through a very difficult period in my life when I left Pitney Bowes after twenty years with the office equipment company. I was also in the middle of my Executive MBA program when I made that decision to leave. One of my professors, Rick Gilkey, noticed the change in my demeanor, attitude, and physical appearance (weight gain). The stress, while obvious to me, was now also obvious to those around me. Rick challenged me to find the leader I once was. He challenged me to get "my mojo" back. Professor Gilkey instructed me to list and to document the behaviors and actions that made me an effective leader. He convinced me to find the elements that brought happiness back into my career and my life. In the last six months of my pursuit of an MBA at Emory University, the seven eLements were born. Once I began to practice them, I did indeed get "my mojo" back. It was after I put the eLements into practice that I began to notice a difference in my relationships, and perhaps just as important, I began to notice a difference in me.

Who should read this book?
This book is for leaders who are serious about learning the art and the skill of effective leadership. This is targeted to individuals who are passionate about creating a culture of trust, caring, and creativity, in which it's acceptable to challenge the status quo. The readers of this book should not be limited to those seeking success in the world of business. Of course, there is value for the young college graduate who is beginning his or her business career, but I hope, perhaps, a young mother who's accepting her first position on the PTA will have a completely different, but equally rewarding, experience by embracing several of the eLements. Perhaps the high school quarterback or student government president will have a different leadership experience by utilizing the techniques in this book. I am confident that the first-time vice president or the newly appointed CEO can also benefit from this information. As a parent, a role that I consider the most important leadership position most of us will ever have, I'm confident a mother or father will build deep and meaningful relationships with their children after mastering the information in this book. I truly believe that aspiring leaders will create a new and rewarding experience for themselves and for those they lead if the eLements become part of their leadership toolbox. Now more than ever, leaders desperately need each of these Seven eLements. Now more than ever, leadership is about forging a connection with those you are fortunate enough to lead.

Leadership is no longer the private domain of corporate executives or civic leaders. I know for a fact that leadership is practiced

Introduction

every day in classrooms, in small town churches, on athletic fields, and yes, in the business world. Politicians, while all recent evidence is to the contrary, claim to have leadership roles in government. The issue with leadership today, however, is that somewhere in our 24/7, media-rich, constant-stimulus world, the message of what it takes to be an effective leader has become cloudy. Fame and money have become the new measuring sticks of success. In my opinion, these are lousy metrics.

This book is for people who want to be a positive influence on others. This book is for people who believe leadership is about serving others. The Seven eLements are for people who care about developing themselves, developing their team members, and bringing out the very best in others. I realize that the previous statements might have just eliminated a few million purchasers of my book. Damn!

Why did I write this book?

I am the CEO of an Atlanta company called LeasePlan USA, which provides financing and vehicle-related services to customers who have large fleets of commercial cars and trucks. I have twenty-five years of sales and management experience, and I have been blessed with the opportunity to learn from several great leaders. I have also gained insight on how not to lead from some pretty pathetic bosses. I've held leadership positions in large global corporations (Dell and Pitney Bowes) and served as a founding member of a small technology company, I2Go, where I was a millionaire on paper for about thirty minutes. After two years in business, I2Go became I2Gone. I have learned that fundamentals of leadership are invariable, regardless of the size of the organization, and I credit each of these roles as extremely valuable learning experiences.

Over the course of the last few years, LeasePlan has been named a "Best Place to Work" by two local papers; named the number one medium-size company to work for in Atlanta, two of the last five years, by *The Atlanta Journal-Constitution;* and recognized by *Fortune Magazine* as one of the "25 Best Medium-Size Companies to Work For" in the United States. I share this as evidence that the material in this book works in the real world. Not only is LeasePlan a great place to work, but the financial performance of the company has been at record levels for several years.

A driving motivation for me to complete this book was to hand a copy to each of my four daughters. But I am also motivated by the fact that I've been delivering a presentation on the Seven eLements for more than a decade, and I have made statements in those presentations about an upcoming book. The Seven eLements are "sticky." People remember these seven attributes of a leader. At a recent presentation in Houston, for example, someone who had seen my presentation and heard me mention the book a few times over the past decade chuckled and commented, "It's a good thing one of the elements is not procrastination." There's always one in every audience. Sometimes the truth hurts, so it's time for me to go to work.

People connect with the Seven eLements. From a corporate vice president to a first-time sales professional; from an eighth-grade student to a class of MBA students, the message seems to resonate. And those who are serious about leadership begin to change their behavior.

What is this book about?

By now, I assume you're wondering, "What are these Seven

Introduction

eLements?" They're as simple as this:

Laugh
Learn
Listen
Language
Lagniappe
Legacy
Love

So simple, yet so powerful when applied.

You might be shaking your head on the "Lagniappe" eLement, but stay with me on this one, as you might end up thinking it's the most powerful of the seven. Perhaps this will be a little something extra that you didn't already know about leadership.

This book is about using the Seven eLements to create a unique team or organizational experience. This experience, for both leader and follower, is built on respect and commitment. This book will challenge some of your beliefs about leadership, and it should have you contemplating new ways of doing things.

The eLements seem to be common sense, but they are certainly *not common practice*.

My dream is that you will **LAUGH** more, and you'll see the humor in everyday events. The message in this book is that you are a student for life, and you should continue to **LEARN** long past graduation day. If you choose to **LISTEN** effectively, and you hear the whispers, your eyes will open to a world full of new possibilities.

My desire is for your **LANGUAGE** to be inclusive, uplifting, and inspiring, with the knowledge that your words have tremendous power. I hope that, as a leader, you will embrace the concept of providing **LAGNIAPPE** and stand out in the world as a person who always does a little something extra. I propose that everyone is capable of building a **LEGACY** of caring and committed young men and women who will continue to build on the foundation that you have created. And lastly, my wish is for **LOVE** to become a regular expression in the workplace and in your home. **LOVE** is accompanied by enthusiasm, empathy, passion, commitment, and of course, change.

I realize that I'm not capable of changing anything for you. I am not that pompous, arrogant, or just plain dumb. Only you have the power to change yourself. I hope that you recognize the truly awesome nature of this power.

I wrote this book in an attempt to help you realize the tremendous influence you have on others. This includes your family, your friends, and your coworkers. From corporate executive to high school student government president, from business titan to local politician, from elementary school teacher to university professor, each has significant influence on those around them, and therefore each should hone their leadership skills. Perhaps the stay-at-home mom who starts her own successful health and fitness business can influence other women to do the same. Each of these leaders can grow by mastering the Seven eLements.

Leadership defined

When reading this book, it's important to share a common definition for leadership.

My definition is simple and straightforward.

Leadership = Influence.

And you influence ALWAYS!

If you're in a position to influence the behavior, thoughts, or feelings of others, then you're in a leadership role. Leadership is

Introduction

both formal and informal, and one does not need a title or position to influence others. Every one of us, on a regular basis, has influence on those around us. By accepting this definition, all of us have the opportunity to lead. All of us have a sphere of influence that is much larger than we believe.

As you read this book, you may find that it's written in a unique style. This was by choice, as I hope you find the informal writing style similar to a conversation or a dialogue, as opposed to a lecture or a monologue. My goal is that you'll finish the book and feel as if you had a conversation with a colleague or a mentor about how to become a more effective leader.

In the next seven chapters, I will introduce you to a formula that I know works. It's a formula that is very simple, but not easy. The awareness of how you influence others is a critical component of success when using the Seven eLements. Remember, leadership is defined as influence, and you influence always!

I am proud to be a part of your leadership journey. I hope you will enjoy this adventure.

Thank you for reading *Seven eLements of Leadership for a New Breed of Leader.*

1

> *"Laugh as much as possible, always laugh. It's the sweetest thing one can do for oneself and one's fellow human beings."*
>
> Maya Angelou

In 2013, LeasePlan USA ranked number one on the list of the "Top Work Places" for mid-sized companies in the city of Atlanta, by *The Atlanta Journal-Constitution*. Later that year, the company was named one of the "25 Best Medium-Size Companies to Work For" in *Fortune* Magazine. For several months after these publications honored our team with this recognition, I received dozens of phone calls every month from job seekers, consultants, and sales professionals. Of all of these phone calls, one stands out as the most memorable.

The "Laughter Coach"

At 7:55 on a Monday morning, my phone rang and the digital display indicated a number that wasn't familiar to me. I usually pick up my own phone, so I answered with my traditional greeting, "Good morning. Mike Pitcher." The voice on the other end of the line sounded like a young man, full of energy, and brimming with optimism on this first day of the workweek. After he introduced himself and congratulated me for LeasePlan's recognition as a great workplace, he stated the purpose of the call.

"I'm a laughter coach, and I can ensure that your company can keep its collective sense of humor," he confidently explained. I was intrigued, and I provided the polite pause he needed to continue his pitch. "Corporate America has lost its ability to laugh, and employees are no longer enjoying their jobs, which can cost you millions in productivity." The words and tone now seemed to be a bit scripted for this "coach."

"A laugher coach?" I questioned, thinking he must be pretty good, as I was sort of chuckling already. Ten minutes later, the call ended, as the young man realized he hadn't done his homework with regard to the company that was on his cold call list. LeasePlan's engagement scores and our employee feedback are testimony to the fact that we laugh a lot at our company. With events such as Thanksgiving turkey bowling, goofy golf, and ping pong played with two-by-fours, LeasePlan team members know how to laugh. In addition, we sponsor events such as the Kentucky Derby, during which members of the LeasePlan team hop aboard oversized bouncing balls and race around traffic cones in the parking lot, wearing the colors of their favorite jockeys.

However, this phone call made me realize the difficult position many businesses must be in when a laughter coach can making a living selling his services. His business model alone leads me to believe that the corporate world must be in big trouble if it needs a consultant to help people laugh at work. How sad is that? Companies are willing to pay a coach to teach their organizations to laugh.

I still laugh at the idea!

Laughter makes us human

You might wonder why I would start a leadership book with a chapter titled "Laugh." Laughter and thumbs are two things that make us human. Laughter is a natural reaction to a funny situation. Funny situations occur practically every day for most people. But society conditions adults to minimize humor and limit it to certain circumstances or environments. A sense of humor is an essential requirement for most leadership positions. Why? Because those who leaders lead—I hesitate to call them followers, but rather supporters, believers, admirers, or enthusiasts—are longing for authenticity.

Regardless of generational differences, most of us are searching for leaders who can be trusted and leaders we can believe in. Authentic leaders show vulnerability and allow others to see their humanity. Laugher is the authenticity that opens the window so others can see inside. Laughter opens the door for meaningful conversations that create meaningful relationships.

In today's fast-paced and rapidly changing environment, it's impossible for one person to be the expert on every subject. The ability to share one's concerns, to question one's assumptions, and to laugh at one's mistakes demonstrates a leader's transparency and authenticity. The omnipotent, all-knowing, expert leader is as out of date as nickel bubble gum.

G'day, mate!

In the late 1990s, I took an international assignment with Pitney Bowes Credit Corporation. I spent the first twenty years of my professional career in sales with the postage meter manufacturer and in management with the company's finance subsidiary. The CEO requested that I evaluate the health and future viability of a financing unit located in Sydney, Australia. As a young man from South Louisiana who didn't even possess a passport, my CEO didn't need to ask me twice.

After only two weeks in Australia, speaking with employees and customers, the reason for the company's poor performance was obvious to me. Issues with employee morale, customer satisfaction, and business execution all pointed at senior leadership. Management was the problem. Senior leadership had very little interaction with frontline employees, and these leaders had no relationship with the company's sales professionals. I sensed little connection between team members. Frontline staff members, however, expressed the view that there was potential in this business unit.

After my return to the United States, I presented my findings to the CEO and other senior leaders in a two-hour, formal presentation. I was confident about my recommendation that the unit should be retained, that the company could indeed be profitable, and that the key to the turnaround would be a clean sweep of existing senior management. As I placed my report in my briefcase, the CEO asked me the question that would change my career. "So Mike, if you truly believe that all it would take to turn the Australia unit around is a change in leadership, would you be willing to take on the role?" Two months later, this southern boy was heading for the Southern Hemisphere.

Laugh

After a few weeks in my new role, I realized that one of the business practices I took for granted in the United States was a novelty in our Australian subsidiary. When our salespeople in the U.S. closed a sale that was leased, we would send the salesperson a pen, a portfolio, or a coffee mug emblazoned with the company logo to celebrate the transaction. Although this might seem like a trivial gift, most sales professionals are by nature very competitive, and when the award is presented in front of their peers, the impact is significant.

I asked my P.A. to make an appointment with a local vendor who could supply our company with a variety of these promotional items. (P.A., in Australia, stands for Personal Assistant, and I was advised not to make the mistake of calling a P.A. a secretary.) My P.A. was a young, very professional, but outspoken redhead named Fiona, who quickly made the appointment for me to meet with a salesman.

Two days after my request, a strapping young Aussie named Ian walked into our office with a box of samples. Ian's box contained dozens of items that could be branded with the company logo and awarded as incentives for outstanding performance. The young salesman informed me that he had one more box of samples in his car, and he would return with it shortly. While Ian was out, I rummaged through his box of goodies and spotted a perfect gift for salespeople who worked and lived in a city full of white sandy beaches. This was going to be easy.

When Ian returned, we started the discussion that I was confident would make his day.

With a smile, I said, "Ian, I already know what I want to buy. I'd like to order some fanny packs!"

With a startled look on his face, he responded, "Excuse me, Mr. Pitcher, what did you say?"

I assumed he was shocked by my readiness to make a purchase without even asking about the price, so I smiled at him and repeated, "I'd like to get some of your highest quality fanny packs!" I added, while placing a hand on his shoulder, "We'll need several hundred, so I'm sure we'll get great pricing."

Much to my chagrin, Ian's response was terse. "Mr. Pitcher, is this a joke?"

"No, it's not a joke. I'll need a couple of hundred fanny packs. In fact, I'd like the company logo, as big as Texas, on every single one." (I was assuming this guy knew how big Texas was.)

Ian, now confused, puffed his chest, stood as tall as his frame could be stretched, and firmly told me, "I don't think this is very funny. I don't know why you called my company, and I don't appreciate you wasting my time. I'll just take my samples and leave."

Now, I was confused. What was this young Aussie talking about? Why should he be upset? With multiple samples of fanny packs in both boxes, I had no idea why we seemed to be disconnected. After all, he was there to sell something, and I was a willing buyer. As the interaction was taking place in an open area of my office, I looked around to see that every single member of my team was head down, looking at papers on their desktops. That was my first tip that something was wrong with this dialogue. I turned to Fiona for some valuable insight. As Ian packed his wares, I stared helplessly at Fiona, hoping for her intervention.

"Fiona, do you have a minute?"

Fiona did not look up from her desk.

"Fiona, pardon me, do you have a minute?"

Fiona slowly raised her eyes from her desk, and I could see that she was biting on her pinky finger and a tear was coming from her

Laugh

left eye. She looked up at me, and with that tear running down her face, began to smile.

"Fiona, what's up?" I realized something was wrong, and she didn't want to tell me what it was.

"Mr. Pitcher, I'm sorry, but I can't say."

"Fiona, remember I'm Mike, not Mr. Pitcher," I reminded her. "And I'm asking you to tell me what I'm missing."

"We just can't laugh at the new boss. We . . . I . . . can't," she replied with a bigger smile.

To which my response was, "Fiona, it's perfectly fine to laugh at the boss. Now tell me what I am missing!"

"Well, boss," the young redhead responded, "in Australia, a fanny is slang for a woman's genitals, and you just asked Ian for two hundred feminine napkins with the Pitney Bowes logo all over each one. As big as Texas, I think you said. The ladies might think it's an okay gift, but the guys just won't see any value in it."

After she said this out loud, the entire office busted out in laughter. I was standing in an office with dozens of people, asking Ian, a young Aussie who probably had all of three weeks selling experience, if he could sell my company hundreds of feminine napkins with the Pitney Bowes logo all over them. I literally laughed so hard that my stomach hurt and I had a difficult time catching my breath. What an idiot these people must have thought I was!

Once the laughter died down and I was able to speak, I apologized to Ian. My new sales advisor on promotional items was later ecstatic over my large order of "bum bags." (In Australia, your rear end is called your "bum," and the pack that straps around your waist is known as a "bum bag.") On that day, all of my team members witnessed a situation that was hilarious, and they realized that it was totally acceptable to laugh at the boss. They realized humor in our office was acceptable. In fact, humor in our office was encouraged.

I was a new leader, in a new country, and made a complete fool of myself in the first month. We laughed and shared stories of other words that I should be aware of that could cause problems in my new homeland. Several team members later made comments about how this event changed and shaped their opinion of me. They realized that I was one of them and we were a team. Fiona told me a few weeks later, "I learned to trust you that day."

> "A good laugh overcomes more difficulties and dissipates more dark clouds than any other one thing."
>
> Laura Ingalls Wilder

The importance of this story is not simply the fact that, as a team, we shared a good laugh with one another. This company was being considered for sale due to profitability concerns. As a team, we began to discuss how to work together to turn the business around. I shared with the team that each person's voice had meaning. Team members realized that we were all in this together. Eighteen months after my arrival down under, our unit was awarded the "Outstanding International Subsidiary" of the year as recognition for reaching 350 percent of target performance in 1995. This was the only time in my career that I was part of a team that achieved its annual financial objectives by July.

Did laughter help? You betcha!

Laughter is good for you

If you consider yourself a practical thinker, and you assume that too much laughter is completely unnecessary and unprofessional, here's something to consider. Laughter is good for your health. There is research that indicates a steady dose of laughter in your life will help you live longer. The Discovery Channel, perhaps taking a page from David Letterman's "Late Night" playbook, offered "Ten Reasons Why Laughing is Good for You."

1. Boosts the immune system
2. Energizes organs
3. Reduces aggression
4. Boosts social skills
5. Helps manage pain
6. Impacts blood sugar levels
7. Provides a burst of energy
8. Improves blood pressure and flow
9. Helps coping skills
10. Decreases stress

The above is a provocative listing of the benefits of laughter; however, one of my personal favorites isn't included: laughter burns calories. It has been found that laughing one hundred times is equivalent to doing ten minutes on a treadmill. So boot up Netflix, watch your favorite comedy, and skip the gym! Of course, I'm kidding. Let me suggest instead that, upon your next visit to the gym, you shouldn't feel guilty when you laugh about the guy in the spandex one-piece.

From a business perspective, I have always found that laughter decreases stress and humor offers a positive course correction in a stressful situation. Although some workplaces do indeed have life or death situations, most of us work in less demanding environments. As a leader, many of your team members will take your lead after the laughter begins. When you laugh, especially at your own expense, they will laugh as well.

One of my favorite titles for a business book is *Why Business People Speak Like Idiots*, by Brian Fugere, Chelsea Hardaway, and Jon Warshawsky. The authors suggest that not only is humor good for you physically, humor is also good for your career. The authors reveal that a significant amount of research has been done on the relationship between an executive's daily use of humor and his or her career advancement and compensation.

> "Fabio Sala, of the consulting firm Hay/McBer, has researched humor extensively. In one study, he interviewed executives from a major corporation and analyzed the interviewees for their use of humor. He then cross-referenced the executives' use of humor with three criteria: the performance bonuses each received, how their peers ranked them, and how they scored on aptitude tests. Sure enough, those who used the most humor were also the ones who got the biggest bonuses, were ranked higher by their peers, and aced the tests."[1]

The authors point out that humor defuses conflict, reduces tension, and puts most people at ease.

Take an opportunity each day to notice the lighter side of your environment. If you have young children, learn a new joke that can be told at the dinner table. Kids are very easily entertained when their parents tell a joke. And remember, even if the joke isn't funny, they get to make fun of your attempt, which can be hilarious if you let it. This is called a win-win situation. If you open this door,

---

1 Brian Fugere, Chelsea Hardaway, and Jon Warshawsky, Why Business People Speak Like Idiots: A Bullfighter's Guide. (New York: Free Press, 2005), 74 – 75.

at work or at home, others will walk right through and have fun with it. Give it a try!

Just what the doctor ordered

In 2001, while living in Atlanta, our family made the decision to have my father live with us after he was diagnosed with Alzheimer's disease. My dad was eighty-two years old and had been living with my mother in New Orleans as her primary caregiver after she had a stroke. You might wonder how any of this could be about laughter or humor. The situation was not funny. As anyone who has lived through the period when their parents' health begins to deteriorate can testify, the days and the decisions are indeed very difficult.

After many consultations with doctors and hours of family discussions, our family made the decision to move my mother to an assisted living facility that offered around-the-clock care and to have my dad move in with me in Atlanta. I also felt that Atlanta would offer the opportunity for better care for my dad's condition. Over the course of several months, I established a relationship with my dad's physician, Dr. Patterson. She not only treated my father, she also spent considerable time with me to explain how this disease would not only change my relationship with him, but would also change my dad's relationship with our entire family.

I remember the sunny June afternoon when my assistant walked into my office and said that there was a call from my dad. I was discussing a new product opportunity with our leadership team, and I asked my assistant to tell my dad that I'd call him right back.

"Your dad says it's an emergency and he needs to talk to you right now!" she said. As I asked the team to give me a few minutes, my imagination ran wild with different scenarios of what would make my dad call me at the office. He had never called before.

"Hey, Pops. What's wrong?"

"Michael, get home right now!" was all he said.

"Dad, is there something wrong at home? Are you okay?"

"Michael, I need you to get your ass home right now!" he yelled into the phone, and then he hung up.

During this thirty-second dialogue, I was reaching for my keys, grabbing my stuff, and running out the door. My house was twenty minutes from the office, so on the way home I called neighbors, my wife, my dad, and no one answered. Driving well over the speed limit, my mind racing, I wondered what kind of emergency this could be. Not sure what to expect as I ran into my house, I was completely shocked to find my dad, feet up on the living room ottoman, watching television.

With a big smile on his face, he greeted me with, "Wow, you're home early. You working banker's hours these days?"

I realized I was yelling at him, but I couldn't stop myself. "Pops, damn it. You called me and told me to come home, said it was an emergency! What's the problem?"

I could see the confusion in his eyes when he responded, "I called you?" It was a question, not a statement. Then his eyes lit up with the memory. "Yes, I did. Yes, I did call you! I remember, I called you!"

"Yes, Dad, you called me. For what? What's the emergency?"

As my eighty-two-year-old father got up, he asked me to wait for a moment, and then he walked into his bedroom. When he returned, my dad held a single sheet of paper, and he told me the reason for the emergency.

"Michael, I have a great joke to tell you! Why is it cool to have Alzheimer's disease?"

"I give up, Pops. Why is it cool to have Alzheimer's disease?"

Now with a great deal of pride, he read the paper word for word. "Because every day you meet brand new people, and on Easter, you can hide your own eggs!" Then he burst out in laughter. I smiled, and I hugged him, and then I began to cry.

The next morning, without an appointment, I sat alone waiting for Dr. Patterson. After I had the opportunity to explain the "crazy behavior" of the previous day, she smiled at me and offered some sage advice. "You won't survive this without a sense of humor." She wasn't talking about my father, but about me.

The good doctor went on to explain several real-life experiences that other patients with Alzheimer's gave their families. Some very sad, some very tragic, and some very, very funny. Her advice to me was simple, and it involved fine-tuning my sense of humor. As I stood up to leave, she walked around to my side of the desk and hugged me. "Mike, laughter, in this situation, is a form of medicine. And it's your medicine."

That advice allowed me to enjoy three incredibly amazing years with my dad. Three years that included many more smiles than tears.

The "F" word is acceptable

No, not that F word. This F word is FUN!

Too many corporate environments have become sterilized institutions where every single day is a replication of the day before. Public classrooms offer cookie-cutter curricula developed by an administrator who has never spent a day in front of students. Many athletic coaches, from youth Pee Wee programs to the college level, have taken the joy and fun out of sports. Adults are told, "Put away your childish ways." Others are advised, "Grow up and smell the coffee." Managers remind employees, "To be taken seriously, you have to be serious." Perhaps this advice should be reconsidered. Herb Kelleher, the legendary founder and CEO of Southwest Airlines, offered some interesting advice when asked about the kind of people who made the airline successful. The famous Texan said, "We hire people who take the business seriously, but not themselves seriously."

Fun is acceptable! Where is it written that the work environment can't be fun? Companies like Southwest Airlines, Google, and Kaiser Permanente have discovered that creating a fun workplace can also create a competitive advantage. These companies have discovered that happy employees create happy customers, and happy customers ensure happy shareholders. By the way, the smart, happy shareholders make sure they retain and reward those happy employees. This is known as a virtuous circle. The model works. Reignite your sense of humor. Take advantage of moments that allow you to bring levity back to offices and classrooms.

Over the course of the past thirty years, I have dressed up as Elvis (and sang), I've donned the cape and leotard of Batman, and I have played the role of a late night talk show host. I have been in a dunk tank and have been hit in the face with multiple types of cream pies. Although I had never smoked cigarettes in my life, I took a few puffs for a music video entitled "I Leased It My Way." (This was a knock-off of Sinatra's "I Did It My Way.") All of this was in good fun and an attempt to bring humor into the workplace.

"Laugh" is the opening chapter to this book because it's so easy. You just have to be open to the opportunity for laughter.

The morning commute:
An opportunity for a great start

I have enjoyed the privilege of presenting the Seven eLements of Leadership to businesses throughout the United States and in the classrooms of universities and colleges. I always encourage those in attendance to provide feedback on the presentation, as I welcome both positive and critical comments about the content. There is one suggestion I make that continues to generate significant positive feedback after every presentation. It has to do with the slightest change in your morning commute.

One of the easiest ways to ensure a great start to any day or project is to focus on the last five minutes before you engage in the activity. For the business leader, this is the last five minutes of your drive to work each morning. For the athlete, it's the last five minutes before going out on the practice field, and for the sales professional, this technique is a change to the last five minutes before you walk into a sales call. Change your channel.

Millions of people on the way to work, on the way to a sales call, or on the way to an athletic event, are influenced by whatever is playing on the radio, the CD, or the digital device. Music is so powerful that it can induce a state of mind. Music has an uncanny ability to make you happy, sad, energized, or emotionally drained.

I suggest that during the last five minutes of your morning commute, or whatever important event you're headed to, you play whatever music you choose that rocks your world. And yes, there is a reason to use the term "rocks your world." The music will be different for each person. Everyone has a certain genre of music that lifts their spirit and energizes them when they need to get their motor running. You'd be amazed at the difference this five-minute ritual can have on your daily routine.

I listen to Toby Keith and Willie Nelson's "Beer for My Horses," and yes, country music is my choice. I turn the volume up so that the windows start to rattle just a bit, and I sing along to most of the song. When the door opens, I feel great about the day. I walk into my office or appointment smiling and confident. I control the last five minutes of my drive—not NPR, not Howard Stern, not the talking heads discussing sports or politics. Even if you use your commute time as an educational opportunity with audiobooks, change your channel for the last five minutes. Music has the ability to change your mood, so why not choose to make your attitude upbeat and positive? The choice is yours.

The Happiness Advantage

I met Shawn Achor in New York in November 2013. LeasePlan invited senior leadership from thirty-two countries to New York City to celebrate our company's 50th anniversary. Shawn Achor is the author of *The Happiness Advantage,* an international bestselling book on the topic of why happiness matters. He is also one of the most talented and gifted public speakers I've ever seen.

Shawn's book provides documented evidence that happiness offers much more than a positive state of mind. As a former Harvard professor who created the famous Happiness Course, Shawn claims that happiness comes before success. He also says that, while there has been a significant increase in the academic research on the subject, most of the business world is uninformed on the topic.

"Despite the academic explosion of positive psychology, its ground-breaking findings are still mostly a secret. When I started in graduate school, the head of the Ph.D. program estimated that the average academic journal article is read by only seven people."[2] Achor dedicates an entire chapter to how happiness gives your brain (and your organization) a competitive edge. He argues against the common belief that success comes first.

"Now, thanks to breakthroughs in the burgeoning field of positive psychology, we are learning that the opposite is true. When we are happy—when our mindset and mood are positive—we are smarter, more motivated, and thus, more successful. Happiness is the center, and success revolves around it."[3]

In fact, researchers Lyubomirsky, King, and Diener compiled the results of more than 200 scientific studies on over 200,000 people and found that happiness leads to success in marriage, health, and friendships, and in particular, our jobs and our careers.[4]

Unfortunately, the corporate world has become a somewhat sterile place. Laughter and fun are considered childish behavior in many corporate and public sector environments. This is truly a tragedy. It's refreshing, however, that many start-up organizations, having grown to thousands of employees, have been able to reintroduce the concept of having fun at work. The ability to laugh, to be happy, and to have fun at work, is rejuvenating. Even high school and college coaches, some in the upper echelon of their chosen sport, are realizing that athletes perform at an optimal level when they're allowed to play the game for fun and for passion.

Laughter exposes our soft side. Laughter heals and soothes. Laughter makes us happy. Laughter is what makes us human. Laughter starts meaningful and trusting dialogue.

The results are in! Laugh! Be happy! Life is a gift!

---

[2] Shawn Achor, The Happiness Advantage (New York: Crown Publishing Group, 2010) 23-24.
[3] Achor, The Happiness Advantage, 45.
[4] Achor, The Happiness Advantage, 52 – 53.

Seven eLements of Leadership

Take Action

Leaders are rewarded when they take action. At the end of each chapter, I'll ask you to take action on what you have learned.

List three ways to incorporate more humor into your life.

1. _____
2. _____
3. _____

As a hint, let me provide the first one. Each week, learn a new joke!

2

LAUGH LEARN LISTEN LANGUAGE LAGNIAPPE LEGACY LOVE

"Leadership and learning are indispensable to each other."

John F. Kennedy

Leadership and learning are inseparable. Today, leaders have been forced to learn to adapt within a constantly changing environment. However, today's leadership roles are different from those of the past. In the new millennium, leaders with an insatiable appetite for knowledge are rewarded above those satisfied with the status quo. Leaders have to be learners.

For the first time in history, current and aspiring leaders must lead five distinctly different generations in the workplace and in communities. According to the author of *Managing the Generational Mix,* the workplace of today is comprised of:

- Traditionalists (1927 to 1945)[5]
- Baby Boomers (1946 to 1964)
- Generation X (1965 to 1984)
- Generation Y (mid-1970s to mid-2000s)
- Millennials (1982 to 2004)[6]

A high school principal, for example, could easily lead a team of educators with several members from each of these generations. These individuals, while viewing the very nature of work differently, have different views on effective leadership. For the principal, understanding these differences is critical to the success of delivering an exceptional education experience for faculty, staff, students, parents, and volunteers.

Early in my career, I heard a speaker advocate a simple three-question performance review. Many in the private sector find it hard to imagine that anything useful could be gained from such a brief review. It consisted of these questions:

1. What did I learn last year?
2. What will I learn this year?
3. What new relationships did I build in the past year?

Questions 1 and 2 clearly allude to the correlation between learning and success. However, in question 3, the concept of learning is perhaps less clear. In an organization, by building new relationships, you can also learn about the work that others do and how others' work impacts the organization as a whole. Building new relationships is all about learning—learning team members' objectives, learning what others do, and learning what is important to them.

---

5 Dr. Jill Novak, "The Six Living Generations in America," Marketing Teacher, accessed July 3, 2015, http://www.marketingteacher.com/the-six-living-generations-in-america/.
6 Phillip Bump, "Here is Where Each Generation Begins and Ends, According to the Facts," The Atlantic, March 25, 2014, accessed July 3, 2015, http://www.theatlantic.com/national/archive/2014/03/here-is-when-each-generation-begins-and-ends-according-to-facts/359589/.

These three questions, although incredibly simple, create a solid learning platform for any aspiring leader. In addition to the aforementioned learning that comes from question 3, there is the additional benefit of learning the names of other team members. Don't underestimate this, as I will go into greater detail in Chapter 5: Lagniappe. Consider asking yourself these same three questions with regard to your own learning and career development.

1. What did I learn last year?
2. What will I learn this year?
3. What new relationships did I build?

Of course, to tighten the timeframe, change year to quarter and then quarter to month.

"What did I learn last month?" is a great question to start with.

Hold yourself accountable for delivering an acceptable answer to each question.

A lifetime of learning

After four years of hard work in high school or college, you graduated and invited your friends and family to the graduation ceremony that recognizes this achievement. Have you ever considered why the ceremony is called commencement? It's referred to as a commencement because it represents the beginning of a new stage in life for the graduate after gaining valuable wisdom and knowledge from an academic institution. Too many graduates, however, treat this day as if it were indeed the end of the learning trail. This view is a big mistake.

LeasePlan USA is in a niche industry—fleet management. When I was approached in 2003 by an executive recruiting firm, I hadn't heard of the company (or the industry, for that matter). In 2004, at my first industry event, I had an opportunity to meet Ed Bobit, one of the stalwarts of the fleet industry. As a novice to the fleet business, I was excited when I walked into the event hall for a keynote speech and I spotted an empty seat next to Ed. When I sat down, he smiled, acknowledged me by my first name, and took out a notebook and pen.

As the speaker gave his presentation, the industry's elder statesman (Ed was in his late seventies at the time) took copious notes. By contrast, I walked into that presentation with the mindset that this was for entertainment value. My attitude was that I had decades of management and leadership experience and this speaker was probably there to entertain the audience for forty-five minutes.

I watched as Ed took notes whenever the speaker stressed an important point. After the session, I commented about Ed's note-taking, and he responded, "Never too old to learn, Mike." Subsequently, I learned that the team of professionals that Ed leads at Bobit Business Media affectionately call him "Coach." This coach obviously leads by example. Over the last ten years, I had multiple conversations with Coach about the importance of a lifetime of learning. Ed Bobit passed away in 2014, but left a legacy of learning and mentoring. He still comes to mind whenever I hear the old cliché, "You are never too old to learn." Thanks, Coach!

Regardless of your status, your level in an organization, or your stage in life, you must be open to learning. In fact, you must possess a passion for learning. Examples of leaders in their chosen fields who are passionate learners are numerous. In professional football, the pregame preparation of both Peyton Manning and Drew Brees are legendary. And how do leaders learn? Learning comes from reading, listening, and doing (experience).

Read, read, read

As a leader, you must become an avid reader. Many leaders of my generation immediately think of a book when told to read. Today, the Internet offers greater opportunities for learning than any physical library on the planet. The Internet has become a "fire hose" of knowledge for anyone willing to drink. My advice to you: drink as much as possible. Sure, you can drown in too much water, and in this analogy, the ocean of information available on the Internet is wide and deep, so be selective.

On any given day, I spend thirty to sixty minutes surfing the Internet. Topics ranging from leading others, to the future of alternative energy, to a myriad of technological breakthroughs interest me. And of course, I keep up with the latest sporting news. I consider all of this learning. In an online search of books on leadership, more than 155,000 search results come up. Trying to read them all is literally impossible, not to mention overwhelming. My point is that the ability to gain knowledge and learn vital information from the Internet is limitless, and with a wide array of mobile applications, this information can be accessed anytime from almost anywhere. The aspiring leader's challenge is more about what to read, as opposed to where to find it.

Make reading a priority and a habit. Start today by making the commitment to invest thirty minutes to an hour a day reading on the Internet or reading a book (possibly recommended by a friend or mentor) with the intent of finding a single nugget of information. I suspect that you will find much more than a single nugget, rather you'll find dozens of strategies that will enhance your leadership skills.

This book includes a suggested reading list that will provide you with several excellent works by leading authors on the subject of leadership. The list not only includes excellent writings on leadership, but also suggests other works related to the Seven eLements.

Learn to listen

The following chapter is dedicated to the subject of listening, but effective listening is so critical to the learning process that I felt it necessary to include the topic in this chapter as well. Early in my career, I worked for a woman named Mary Maarberg of Pitney Bowes. Mary had a brilliant finance mind, but very little sales experience. During the early weeks of our relationship, Mary said, "Mike, I know very little about sales. I don't think you know a lot about finance and treasury, so let's make a deal. I will teach you about finance, if you teach me about sales. Do we have a deal?" I thought to myself, "This woman already knows how to close!" I have always respected this approach to our relationship, one that was built on each of us learning from the other. In addition to financial acumen, Mary offered me another learning opportunity. That lesson was that there is a time to speak and there is a time to listen.

After a meeting with bankers, something that was completely foreign to me, Mary pulled me aside to offer her sage advice. "There is a time to talk and a time to listen. Until I ask you a question in these meetings, you need to simply listen." This seems to be so simple; however, for many new leaders, it's not easy. Many leaders are trained to respond to every possible statement or question that an employee, customer, peer, or even a spouse makes or asks. But there are times when it's best to simply listen. A mentor once told me, "If you are speaking, you are not learning." There are many situations when it is best to *listen and learn*.

In most major metropolitan areas, the average commute time

is about an hour each way. This is an excellent opportunity to enroll in what I call a "mobile university." Audiobooks can provide a wealth of information. If you pick a single day a week to convert the time you spend getting from point A to point B to a learning experience, by the end of the year you are fifty hours smarter in whatever subject you choose. But don't forget, it's a great idea to end the last five minutes of your commute with the music that "rocks your world" (see Chapter 1).

Just do it!

Neither a book, nor a CD, nor a DVD, nor the Internet could prepare you for a simple learning experience that almost all of us have had: learning to ride a bike. Thousands of illustrations, an explanation of balance, a fantastic YouTube video, or listening to the instructive words of your overzealous parents could not take the place of the breathtaking experience of pedaling your first bike. By doing it yourself, you learned how to ride a bike. In addition, when you fell (and most of us did), you also learned another valuable lesson. That lesson was when you fall, get back up. There is a valuable lesson in taking action—just do it!

Experts agree that experiential learning is the most valuable form of education. The act of doing far outweighs any other form of learning. In the corporate world, although new sales representatives may do dozens of role plays, they always remember their first real face-to-face sales call (with a real prospect who can spend real money). In the education sector, many teachers have confessed that nothing can fully prepare you for your first day in the classroom, standing in front of twenty-five children and introducing yourself as their teacher. Mock trials are no replacement for the experience of a trial before a jury for a young attorney.

Career counselors recommend that an individual look for opportunities in an organization to learn a myriad of skills. To do this, leaders might have to take lateral rather than vertical moves to gain valuable knowledge about how an organization works. Be open to new learning experiences, and think of your career as a marathon, not a sprint. It's quite common for a well-rounded leader to have had stints in sales, finance, and information technology. Each of these positions, among others, affords the opportunity for invaluable learning and leadership growth.

No matter how many lateral or upward moves you make in your career, remain focused on keeping in contact with those who pay the salaries of everyone in the organization—customers and clients. As leaders rise in an organization, they tend to move farther away from direct interaction with clients and frontline service providers. This distance is dangerous. Maintain some connection with frontline team members, clients, customers, or partners. With every promotion in your leadership journey, you can become more and more insulated from where the profits are made.

The same is true for other leadership positions. As you rise in the leadership role, remain connected to those who make up the valuable foundation of the organization, whether volunteers, students, parents, or others. Value what you can learn from everyone on your leadership journey.

Learning and the Internet

Although I have just explained the importance of reading, listening, and doing for your personal development, the importance of the Internet as a learning tool must be addressed. The Internet has become a valuable tool for viewing dynamic content. As an aspiring leader, you can be exposed to the teachings of Bill Gates, Sheryl

Sandberg, Tony Robbins, or John Wooden, among others. Professors from some of the most prestigious educational institutions in the world are now sharing their knowledge in videos of lectures that are posted on the Internet.

One example of this exceptional opportunity to learn online from various outstanding leaders is called the TED Talk. TED is an acronym for Technology, Entertainment, and Design. TED is a nonprofit organization that brings together speakers who present on almost every topic in a concise presentation, generally eighteen minutes or less. (For a real chuckle, watch as the organizers try to keep the dynamic Tony Robbins to the eighteen-minute limit.) TED talks have become a phenomenon across the globe and are now broadcast via the Internet in one hundred languages.

Invest twenty minutes per week watching these dynamic talks for your own personal development. Search "25 TED Talks That Will Make You a Better Leader." The list of featured presenters includes Dan Pink (motivation), Amy Cuddy (body language), and Shawn Achor (happiness).

If you enjoy learning through lecture, don't miss this opportunity to expand your knowledge. The site is www.TED.com.

Three things

In my decades in business, there is one question that new and aspiring leaders ask me time and again: "What do I need to learn?" Ask a dozen exceptional leaders this question, and you will probably get a dozen answers. Over the last decade, my answer has amounted to these three things:

1. Learn to embrace change.
2. Learn that your attitude is everything.
3. Learn the importance of diversity.

You might be thinking, "What about public speaking skills or executive presence?" Of course presentation skills and having a visible presence are important, among other valuable leadership traits. The three things that I propose you learn focus on your attitude about conditions you will face as a leader.

Learn to embrace change

Change is a tsunami that no one can stop.

As I write this chapter, I am on a flight from London to Atlanta. Yesterday in London, cab drivers brought traffic in a part of the city to a complete standstill. Traffic in London is among the worst in the world to start with, but the cab drivers blocked a major thoroughfare in downtown London in protest of the Uber web application being used on mobile phones.

Nine months ago, a sixty-five-year-old colleague of mine showed me the app on his iPhone and told me how much he loves it. Since discovering the Uber application, he and his wife no longer drive to dinner. He can enjoy a drink, perhaps several, and access Uber so a driver will pick him up from any corner in Atlanta and drive him home.

The London cab drivers, however, may have done their cause more harm than good. Due to this public display, every medium from print to television and, of course, digital media covered this story. Apparently, millions of Brits, wondering what all the fuss is about, have gone to the site and downloaded the app. Oops! This disruptive technology will not be stopped by a London traffic jam on a Thursday afternoon. The adoption of this technology, however, might be sped up by bringing it to everyone's attention. Thank you very much!

There are thousands of examples of change that impact both your personal and your professional life. Mobile computing has impacted the way you bank, shop, and interact with friends and family. Social media is changing so fast that companies that were once the Internet darlings of the new millennium are struggling to keep up with the dazzling technology of new ventures. Companies that were known for their disruptive technology just a few years ago are now being disrupted.

Technologists and futurists believe that, in the next twenty-five years, technology will change at a rate five to seven times faster than the previous twenty-five years. To fully understand how this statement will impact you as a leader who will still be working and leading in 2040, it's best to give this some perspective. Asking today's leaders what the world of technology will look like in the future is analogous to asking your great-great-grandparents—when they were your age—what the world of communications and technology would look like in 2015. It is difficult to comprehend or predict how technology will impact our lives.

In my own industry of transportation, companies are developing a "driverless car." In fact, I have seen such a vehicle successfully navigate a short track. Five years ago, no one even spoke of this as a concept. New entrants to this market, such as Google and Apple, will certainly have the attention of today's automotive market share leaders, Toyota and General Motors.

The rapid speed of technological change, however, is not the critical point. The critical point is that leaders need to embrace change or they run the risk of being left behind in its wake.

Technology is not the only change that today's (and tomorrow's) leaders will face. Issues as simple as business attire, flexible work weeks, and physical work space are changing for most business leaders. Many large corporations struggle with the casual environment that is being offered to young professionals. At LeasePlan, we've found one of the most important benefits to a majority of our team members is the ability to wear jeans several days a week. Team members have stated that not only does the casual dress policy lead to a more relaxed atmosphere, but it also leads to a financial benefit through reduced costs for dry cleaning.

Recently, one of my daughters, while visiting our home for the weekend, slept in and was running late for work on Monday morning. When she came down the stairs in exercise shorts and a t-shirt, I assumed she would change before going to her job. "No," she said, as she grabbed her keys. "We are totally casual, Dad. Most people dress like this every day." (By the way, her company is a "best place to work" in Atlanta and is also recognized as a "fastest growing company" in the city.)

The technology we use at home and at work, the physical workplace, and the definition of work itself, are all changing at a rapid pace. Today's successful leader must be attuned to these changes.

Learn that your attitude is everything

Your attitude, including your attitude toward constant change, is a weapon that only you can bring to bear. You are completely and solely responsible for your attitude.

Zig Ziglar, one of the pillars of the self-development movement, said it best when he said, "Your attitude, not your aptitude, determines your altitude in life." Baby boomers have heard this catchy phrase for decades, but for young leaders today, this could be new material. Regardless of your tenure in leadership, this statement still rings true. For the vast majority of leaders, attitude is the foundation of success. Men and women who are well known on the leadership landscape have survived massive failures in their businesses and careers. Failure did not slow them down.

Michael Jordan's inability to make the cut on his high school basketball team is well documented. Elon Musk—the founder of Tesla Motors—and his flirtation with bankruptcy and financial ruin have been the subject of multiple television documentaries. From a historical perspective, it would be difficult to find a former president of the United States with more political losses than Abraham Lincoln. For many athletes, business executives, political leaders, and entrepreneurs, the foundation of their success is indeed their own attitude and perseverance. Their attitude about every failure and obstacle remains the same: "The failure was a temporary setback, but I will succeed."

Over the course of more than three decades, I have been blessed with the opportunity to work with hundreds of amazing leaders. These men and women were intelligent, insightful, charismatic, and passionate. Some were blessed with great vision and foresight, and others had technical and financial skills that still baffle me today. When I think of the great leaders, those who others, including myself, would follow without question, I realize each of these leaders had one thing in common: a positive attitude. In fact, it was a positive "can do" attitude.

When circumstances are the most bleak, which leader do you want to follow—the one who says, "I'm not sure we'll make it" or the leader who says, "We can do this!" and proceeds to suggest how you can be successful together? Most people want to follow someone who sees some light at the end of the darkest tunnel. Leaders simply don't quit.

The importance of a positive attitude is not only critical when times are tough. Most people, in good times and bad, want to be around leaders who view the world through an optimistic lens. Why? These individuals are simply more pleasant to be around. You can probably think of a friend, family member, or coworker whose attitude nearly sucks the life out of you every time you're around them. Complaints can range from how bad they're feeling, to how lousy their job is, to what a loser they're dating (for years), to how no one comes to visit, to how bad the quality of the free coffee is. You might continue to maintain these relationships even though time spent with these people drains you of energy and passion. When these individuals are coworkers or friends, sever the relationship. If these energy suckers are family members, limit your exposure or have a discussion about how the time spent is taking a toll on your attitude. These relationships are difficult to break, but you will benefit in the end.

In their best-selling book, *How Full Is Your Bucket?*, authors Tom Rath and Don Clifton suggest that all of us go through life wearing an imaginary bucket on our hip.[7] This mystical bucket is constantly being filled or emptied by the numerous interactions you have every day with family, friends, and coworkers. The positive and negative interactions that occur on a daily basis are the filling or the emptying of your bucket. Can you see the imagery of this analogy? People in your life are constantly walking by and filling you up with positive messages. In contrast, there are individuals who continually drain your bucket by leaving you less emotionally fulfilled than you were prior to meeting them.

Both Rath and his grandfather Don Clifton worked for the Gallup organization and collected data related to positive psychology. The authors claim that we experience approximately 20,000 "moments" each day that lead to the development of our own self-

---

[7] Tom Rath, Donald O. Clifton, How Full Is Your Bucket? (New York: Gallup, 2004).

image. According to their research, it's important for an individual to be aware of the dual impacts of daily interactions. In other words, are you a bucket filler, or do you tend to empty the buckets of those you interact with? In addition, what are the impacts to your own bucket through the daily interactions of your colleagues, your family, and your friends?

Attitude is a choice. There are days that, by 10 a.m., there have been multiple attacks on my positive mental attitude. I fight back, and more often than not, I win the battle because I choose to be happy. I live in the greatest country in the world. I have four intelligent and beautiful daughters and a wife I'm madly in love with, and I am pretty healthy. (Okay, so I could afford to lose a few pounds.) I am a blessed man, and I choose to be happy.

Your attitude is your responsibility and your choice.

For the past ten years, I've started every morning with a mental ritual that has helped put me in the right frame of mind. I ask myself a simple question:

"What three things make me happy today?"

Then I mentally list the three things. I could list dozens of things that make me happy, but every morning I come up with three. The new picture of my grandson sent to my iPhone, the new account we won at LeasePlan, and a great dinner I prepared on the grill the night before. The next morning, the three could include finishing a great book, helping a friend with a problem, and the fact that my wife was feeling a little amorous the night before. I'm confident that you get the picture. You shouldn't have a problem creating a list of three things that make you happy; you just have to consciously do it. Stop reading for just a moment, and mentally create your list. What are three things that you're happy about right this moment? Seriously! Put the book down and name three things that make you happy.

Smile. You are blessed.

The three things that make you happy don't have to be huge events in your life. The process is about recognizing how truly fortunate you are. Try it. For one week, when you wake up, state out loud three things that make you happy that day. I'll give you one for starters: God blessed you with another day; you woke up! If you're healthy, you can easily start with that same blessing each and every day. An attitude of gratitude is truly an amazing emotion.

Learn the importance of diversity

Ask most leaders about the concept of diversity, and you'll get politically correct answers about gender diversity, ethnic diversity, or lifestyle diversity. Diversity is so much more than this. From a business perspective, diversity is about the opportunity to bring people together who have had diverse life experiences which will contribute to better decision-making for the group, team, organization, or company. Diversity can relate to gender, ethnicity, age, or lifestyle, but at a base level, it's about diversity of life experience. As a fifty-seven-year-old, white male from South Louisiana, I will never see the world through the eyes of a twenty-two-year-old African American woman from New York. And by the way, this woman would never be able to see the world through my eyes. Learning to appreciate and accept that there are benefits to our diverse life experiences is where harnessing the power of diversity begins.

In a 2014 study by the Forbes Insight Group, diversity is noted as a key driver of innovation and a component for business success on a global scale.[8] The study also states that a diverse and inclusive

---

[8] "Global Diversity and Inclusion: Fostering Innovation Through a Diverse Workforce." Forbes Insight Group, 2014.

workforce is crucial for companies that want to attract and retain top talent. With regard to leadership's role as it relates to diversity initiatives, the study finds that responsibility for the success of a company's diversity efforts lies clearly on the shoulders of senior management.

During my career at Pitney Bowes, I was considered a "high potential" executive. This designation afforded me the opportunity to participate in several leadership development programs. I attended sessions created and delivered by the Wharton Business School, Babson Business School, and Emory University. Fresh out of one of these programs, I attended a session for senior leadership to discuss the composition of a task force being formed to evaluate a future growth strategy. As I looked at the names on the list for consideration, I realized that there were no black men on the list. This was my chance to prove the money spent on my personal development was a good investment.

"I think we should put Zack P. on the list," I said. I was confident that this statement would please Peggy, the African American vice president of the HR department. I even flashed her a winning smile so she would know that I knew she was proud of me.

"Really? Zack? Why would you suggest him?" she inquired.

Why would Peggy challenge me on this?

"Peggy, I just think we need a guy like Zack on this task force. He would be an asset!"

She didn't relent. "Why do you think he would be an asset?"

I wondered if she was testing me. With my smile now gone, I said, "Because he's a bright, young guy, and we could use the diversity on the team." Although it was a statement, the tone of my voice got higher at the end, almost as if my assertion was a question awaiting her approval.

"Diversity?" she shot back. "Do we really need diversity on this team?"

She had me on my heels now, and I was confused. "Yes, shouldn't the team be diverse?"

"I agree, but why?"

"Because Zack is black, and we need someone black." I stammered.

And then her face changed. That's when I heard the words that any young, aspiring leader *never* wants to hear. "You just don't get it, do you?" She continued, "Diversity is not about race, or gender, or age. It's about the diversity of life experiences that each of us has. We want and need diversity of life experiences to ensure that we make the best business decisions possible. That's why Zack is a great choice, not just because he's a black man."

Wow! Ouch! I still remember the sting of this discourse, but it was also an amazing learning experience for me.

My diversity story

In 2012, I had the opportunity to participate in a leadership program called Leadership Atlanta. The program is the oldest and longest running municipal leadership development program of its kind in the United States. On an annual basis, more than eighty men and women of diverse professional backgrounds come together for this nine-month leadership experience.

At the opening session of this program, each participant was introduced by former graduates of Leadership Atlanta. I was amazed at the talent, intelligence, and success of the members of my class. It was a very humbling experience, and I continually asked myself, "What am I doing here?" In addition to realizing that this was the most successful collection of individuals I had ever been around, I also realized it was the most diverse in gender, age, ethnicity, and religious beliefs. I later realized that this was not by accident; it was by design.

Early in the program, we attended a two-day, mandatory session entitled "Race Weekend." Our class was divided into two groups that would attend Race Weekend A and Race Weekend B, due to the large size of the class. Out of respect for the Leadership Atlanta experience, and for the facilitator, Al Vivian of Basic Diversity, I cannot reveal the details of the seminar. Suffice it to say, it changed my life. As a veteran leader of two large corporations, I had attended several diversity programs, but none of them had as profound an impact on me as this Leadership Atlanta two-day session. The program was centered on race diversity, and in the city of Atlanta, as in many large metropolitan areas throughout America, the subject is more often swept under the rug, rather than discussed in meaningful conversations.

As we addressed the issues of black and white in the city of Atlanta, I became very aware of the divide that separates us with regard to race. I explained to this group of strangers an experience I had with a colleague, who happened to be black. Years earlier, while participating in a sales training event in Los Angeles, I found myself amid a group of about eight male colleagues—all of whom I knew fairly well. When one of our black male colleagues was the punchline of a racial joke made by a senior leader, I laughed with the others. I did nothing. My lack of action, and backbone, has bothered me for years. I spoke with my colleague later and explained that "I knew how he felt" and it was an unfortunate experience. His response was quick and terse: "Bullshit. You will never know what it's like to be a black man in America." He was dead right. I was dead wrong. Leadership takes courage. Standing up for what's right and just is sometimes a lonely experience. But in the end, it's the right thing to do.

Racial diversity is a complex and controversial subject in America. The only way our country can reach its true potential is to have an open, honest, inclusive, civilized dialogue about the issues of race. This is how learning, awareness, and change can begin.

One of the first steps in bridging the racial divide for the Leadership Atlanta group was a challenge by our group leader. Al Vivian charged each of the "white folks" in the room to find one or two "Race Ambassadors" who would be willing to discuss their experiences as African Americans in Atlanta. We were to engage in a meaningful dialogue about the challenges faced every day by someone who is black. I identified two ambassadors—one male, one female, both trusted advisors—who shared their insights with me.

My black colleagues have taught me that all people wish to be looked upon as equals, with expectations that they will rise to the occasion as their abilities, intellect, desire, and experience allow. Most people do not want a handout—or even a hand up. They want the same opportunities as everyone else to demonstrate their unique talents in an environment that doesn't judge them by the color of their skin, or their ethnic garb, or their religious beliefs, or the spelling of their name, or their zip code. The hatred and preconceived notions born of racism too often result in a dangerous disconnect and withholding of basic human rights. America is better than that. In this 21st century, we have learned from our muddied and bloodied history, and so we must do more to create diverse forums so we can all learn from each other and progress as a nation.

I am confident that I have grown as an individual. I am also confident that I still have a long way to go (and grow).

This diversity experience was personal for me, and it was indeed about racial diversity. There are misperceptions about race, ethnicity, sexual orientation, age, and gender. Until you begin to have meaningful dialogue with individuals who are different from you, you might never have the chance to expand your relationships outside of your existing comfort zone. In other words, you will eliminate relationships that could possibly enhance the quality of your life.

Many corporate diversity courses are created and executed to check a box. I urge you to look deeper and to do more. Whether you associate with any group, are black or white, male or female, gay or straight, I urge you to reach out to begin these discussions with team members who you trust in the workplace, with your own family members, or with friends in your neighborhood.

Take Action

1. What new method of learning will you commit to? _____

_____

_____

_____

2 What action will you take to embrace change in your daily routine? _____

_____

_____

_____

3. How can you expand your sphere of influence to include new diverse relationships? _____

_____

_____

_____

3

"Man's inability to communicate is a result of his failure to listen effectively."

Carl Rogers

One of the most important, yet least discussed, skills of an effective leader is listening. High school and university courses are easy to find for someone wanting to improve in the areas of debate or public speaking, but to find a dedicated course in listening skills would be a challenge. According to Glenn Liopis, a leadership contributor for *Forbes Magazine,* less than 2 percent of all professionals have had formal education to improve listening skills and techniques. In addition, according to Liopis, humans generally listen at a 25 percent comprehension rate.[9] This is unfortunate, as listening is a crucial element of leadership effectiveness. Far too many leaders spend too much time talking and not enough time listening.

Admittedly, I have faced my own challenges in this area as a leader. Throughout my career, I have concentrated more on my ability to speak—effectively giving instruction, direction, supervisory comment, and evaluation—and less on listening (except to make sure others are listening to me at critical moments). Old-school leadership training suggests that good communication begins with being able to speak well and get your message across quickly. *The Seven eLements* flips the script and places listening at the top of the communication grid.

Unfortunately, I brought my old-school leadership thinking about listening into my interactions with my family. As a husband and father, I've had to learn that our family bonds are stronger, and much more gets accomplished, when we listen to one another. But that took years, and I'm still improving in this area. My daughters don't miss a chance to let me know I still have work to do. In fact, when I began to work on the outline for this book, I shared the content with my children. Lauren, my oldest daughter, seemed particularly interested in the chapters that I had outlined. "Dad, I really like the content, but I think you should consider one additional chapter."

Proud of her interest and intrigued by the notion of additional content, I continued the conversation. "What element of leadership do you feel I left out?"

"Rocket science," she proclaimed.

---

9 Glenn Liopis, "6 Ways Effective Listening Can Make You a Better Leader," Forbes Magazine, May 20, 2013.

"Are you talking about intelligence, as in 'smart as a rocket scientist'?"

"Nope, just a chapter on rocket science," she responded with a bit of a grin.

Obviously, I was confused by this dialogue. As a new chapter on rocket science seemed utterly ridiculous to me, I made an attempt to explain the power of alliteration. "Lauren, can't you see the whole L thing I have going on? Laugh, Learn, Listen—"

She interrupted with a bigger smile. "Rocket science!"

"Why in the world would I include a chapter in a leadership book about rocket science?"

Her response gave me no further insight. "I think you should include a chapter on rocket science!"

"Lauren, I don't know anything about rocket science," I declared in a louder tone.

"Dad, you don't know anything about listening, but you're writing a chapter on it!"

Touché to my eldest child. I realize that I am still a work in progress. And in the spirit of full disclosure, this eLement is the most difficult for me.

Listen to understand—Effective listening

Those who have attended training in sales and in management know that the majority of the instruction is about what to say and how to say it. Budding leaders are told over and over again that "there is power in words," meaning the words you speak. But what about the power of listening? And more to the point, the power of effective listening.

Effective listening means not only hearing and listening to the words that someone speaks, but also looking for additional meaning from clues in the speaker's voice tones and messages sent through body language. In essence, effective listening is the beginning of understanding.

Listening and fully understanding the views and concerns of others allows meaningful communication to occur. Your success as a leader requires mastering your listening skills. When you truly listen as a leader, you show empathy and compassion, and in the process you build relationships based on trust and transparency.

The benefits of effective listening are critical in areas other than the professional arena. By listening effectively, you learn what motivates and inspires those around you. The leader who masters this skill also becomes finely attuned to learning, as listening skills are the foundation of learning.

Listen to participate—Active listening

I work with several executives who enjoy listening to music as they work. I am told by my colleagues that this practice allows them to relax and to be more productive. I characterize this as passive listening. In fact, I would venture to bet there are times that the listener doesn't even know the song or the artist they're hearing.

Contrast this type of experience with active listening, when as the receiver, you are actively engaged in the communication process. In essence, you're an active participant with another person (or several people), not only verbally, but vocally and visually. Your focus is on more than just the words being spoken to you. With active listening, you participate by connecting the speaker's words with the speaker's body language and tone to understand the total message. Active listening is an attempt to get the full meaning of the communication.

There are several keys to becoming an active listener who participates fully in a conversation:
- Start with an open mind.
- Pay attention.
- Prove you are engaged.
- Don't interrupt.
- Listen with your eyes *and* your ears.
- Try to *feel* what the speaker is saying.
- Eliminate distractions.
- Practice, practice, practice.

Start with an open mind

Many people enter conversations with some preconceived notions about the other person. You might assume that those who want a conversation with you have a hidden agenda. You have already decided what they want, and often, you've decided how you will respond to their request or statement. This approach could open the door for misunderstanding, unfair judgement, and missed opportunities for praising or thanking others. Instead of beginning conversations behind the mask of assumptions, make an attempt to start fresh. Begin each conversation with an open mind and try to envision what positive outcomes are possible through this conversation.

> "Most people do not listen with the intent to understand, they listen with the intent to reply."
>
> Stephen Covey

When I joined LeasePlan as Executive Vice President of Sales in

2003, I learned that an internal candidate for the position would be a direct report. I met a few people in the organization who described Bryan, a twenty-year industry veteran, as a person with a "hidden agenda." During our first year of working together, my communication with Bryan was somewhat guarded, and I kept listening for clues to this "hidden agenda." Because of this, I wasted twelve months of productive relationship building. I kept waiting for that "gotcha" moment that would prove my preconceived notions were right. It didn't happen.

Bryan is one of the most professional, detailed, and passionate sales executives I've had the privilege of working with. His hidden agenda was fabricated in a few people's minds, and I let that cloud my view of a person I had never met. Dumb. Dumb. Dumb. Allow yourself the opportunity to form your own opinions about others through your interactions and conversations with them.

Pay attention

This advice might sound like common sense, but the sad fact is that paying attention to the person who is speaking to you isn't common practice these days. Our world has become saturated with stimuli that compete for your attention. Not only that, we have become so proud of our ability to multitask that we've all but lost the ability (and dare I say, desire) to focus on one thing or one conversation at a time. As a leader, you cannot afford the mistake of not paying attention during critical conversations with team members.

People want to be heard and understood. They want to know that you value their input. You demonstrate this to them when you pay attention to their comments, concerns, and suggestions.

Demonstrate to others that you are interested in listening to them by being present. Be there. Be in the moment. I don't suggest that this is easy. You are the only person who controls your level of attentiveness. This decision is yours to make. When you invest in a meaningful conversation, others will value the time you invest.

Be engaged

Being engaged in a conversation means responding and reacting to the speaker's cues so he or she knows you are listening and involved in the conversation. Make an attempt to use any of the following in your next conversation:

- Look the speaker in the eyes.
- Nod your head occasionally in agreement.
- Lean into the conversation.
- Smile occasionally.
- Maintain an open posture (crossed arms can send a negative message).

If appropriate, ask clarifying questions to demonstrate to the speaker that you are actively listening and that you care about understanding what he or she is saying.

Taking notes also demonstrates to the other person that you're listening to get understanding. Note-taking also benefits you. It has been well documented that note-taking can increase your ability to retain information by up to 25 percent, and when you review your notes within twenty-four hours, retention increases even further.

Being engaged benefits you in one-on-one conversations and in group interaction. When I attended a marketing class at the University of Georgia with one of my daughters, I was amazed to sit in class with more than 250 students. The professor used PowerPoint slides, and her oratory skills were quite impressive. Unfortunately, she didn't engage the students throughout much of her presentation. At the beginning of the lecture, a large percentage of the class seemed disengaged and lacked interest in the content. Later, when several students started to ask questions, a lively dialogue began and the energy in the class noticeably changed (for the better, I might add). Once a dialogue started and the professor listened to the questions, other students also became engaged in the process, sometimes asking a follow-up to another student's question. This is just one example of how the behavior of the listener can have a very positive impact on the interaction between people. Leadership is about influence, and active listeners do indeed influence a conversation.

Don't interrupt

Like most people, you've felt the frustration in a conversation when someone is constantly interrupting and not allowing you to finish. This behavior is often the expression of one person trying to exert or obtain power in a conversation. If the power-grabber is you, stop this negative behavior.

Oftentimes, men have a problem with interrupting others in a conversation. I realize that I am painting with a very wide sexist brush, but I'm willing to take the risk. Many men, and I include myself in this group, want to immediately "fix" whatever the issue is. While listening to someone present an issue or a problem, the male mind immediately begins to formulate the solution to this problem. We're perched and ready to display our problem-solving prowess—if only the speaker would take a breath. Many times we think, "To hell with a pause, I'm jumping right in." As the father of four daughters, I have to confess to being told on multiple occasions, "Dad, I just need you to listen to me."

In my professional life, I am prone to making this mistake. I have colleagues who have presented complex business issues for consideration, and before the presentation is finished, I've offered a solution. When this happens, members of my team often respond with a trigger, such as, "Please let me finish," and I realize my mistake. My position as the CEO does not give me the power to interrupt others simply to offer my opinions or solutions. That kind of behavior would likely cause others to avoid having conversations with me or sharing their ideas in my presence, making me an ineffective leader. In the last several years, I've become aware of my tendency to interrupt, and I continually work to eliminate this counterproductive behavior. Again, I am a work in progress.

Not interrupting others takes practice. Make a commitment that during your next conversation with a family member, team member, or business colleague, you will refrain from interrupting. Concentrate on listening to the speaker. Don't finish any sentences for them, and don't cut the speaker off. Ask questions for clarity, and allow the speaker to finish his or her thoughts. Listen for a natural pause if you have a question or need clarification.

In the beginning, this might require a muzzle, or you might find you'll actually have to place your finger over your lips to keep from speaking. That's okay. Perhaps you have been interrupting others for so long that some people believe they can't finish their own sentences without you. Take a break and allow them to finish. Notice the change—in yourself and in the other person—and smile when it happens. If you tend to be the dominant speaker in a conversation, trust me, this is going to be very difficult. The initial anxiety you experience by not interrupting others will be well worth the quality of conversations you start to enjoy.

Listen with your ears *and* your eyes

In the same way that your body language is constantly communicating with others, the body language of the person speaking to you offers visual clues, so pay close attention. Is there an openness about his or her posture that invites you to further the conversation? Watch the eyes and the lips of the speaker for meaning behind the message.

An individual's eyes will often tell you much more than the words. Fear, happiness, anxiety, and stress can be seen in someone's eyes, even when their words communicate a different message. The lips can indicate anger or frustration. Folding one's arms and leaning way back in a chair is usually a message that this person is withdrawing from the conversation. Pay attention to non-verbal clues that provide additional insight into how a person is perceiving the conversation.

Try to *feel* what the speaker is saying

When you are engaged in a deep, meaningful conversation, there are times when what is not said is more important than what is said. Perhaps there is a word unspoken that speaks louder than any word that's spoken. Picking up on this takes listening from the heart and feeling what the speaker is saying.

In both business and personal conversations, the speaker may only be saying the words that he or she is comfortable stating out loud. There could be deep-seated emotional issues, such as disappointment, fear, sadness, or grief, that aren't easy to talk about. In these situations, allow your heart to feel this person's emotions at that moment. Try to feel what the speaker means while they are speaking.

Psychiatrist Mark Goulston dedicates a section of his book *Just*

Listen to this concept. The section titled "Make the Other Person Feel Felt" addresses the emotional connection that occurs when the speaker gets the sense that the listener actually feels what the speaker feels.

> "Making someone feel felt simply means putting yourself in the other person's shoes. When you succeed, you can change the dynamics of a relationship in a heartbeat. At that instant, instead of trying to get the better of each other, you "get" each other and that breakthrough can lead to cooperation, collaboration, and effective communication."[10]

Goulston further explains that once the person you're communicating with feels felt, you will find it easier to communicate your request, such as more work from a coworker, a decision from your coach, or a negotiation with a sponsor of your organization. When someone feels felt, that person will give you less attitude, less obstruction, and more support.

Eliminate distractions

So much of today's communication is digital. Smartphone owners between the ages of eighteen and fifty-five send approximately 4,700 text messages each month, according to a 2013 report by Experian. That doesn't even include the nearly 3,400 texts they receive. And these are 2013 numbers![11] Several recent studies indicate that many adults, perhaps of the baby boomer generation and earlier, miss the face-to-face interaction so common in days gone by.

---

10 Mark Goulston, Just Listen: The Secret to Getting Through to Absolutely Anyone (New York: American Management Association, 2010), 78.
11 Alex Cocotas, "Chart of the Day: Kids Send a Mind Boggling Number of Texts Every Month," BusinessInsider.com, March 22, 2013, accessed July 3, 2015, http://www.businessinsider.com/chart-of-the-day-number-of-texts-sent-2013-3.

Advances in technology have improved efficiency for business, civic, and nonprofit leaders. Technology now allows you to remain in 24/7/365 contact with customers and clients, constituents, family, and staff. Voicemail, text messages, email, and photographs are instantly accessible on a variety of mobile devices. The majority of this communication is now being delivered by the smartphone or tablet. I would argue that today's technological advances are both a blessing and a curse.

The constant bombardment of electronic communication distracts from the critical task of effectively communicating with those directly in front of you. Although these new technologies have many benefits, our ability to focus is becoming diminished.

Consider dining out with a family member or a business colleague who has requested your time so they can share some important news. The restaurant you select has multiple televisions that provide the latest news and sports for your viewing pleasure as you dine. Couple that with the constant presence of your smartphone, and you can imagine how focused you might be on the other person.

When having face-to-face discussions, try to eliminate distractions such as the telephone, email, text messages, or others nearby. Do your best to concentrate on the person you are speaking with. Turn off your cell phone, position your computer screen so it's not facing you. Choose to concentrate on this one conversation at this one point in time. This single decision will allow you to dramatically increase your level of understanding.

Practice, practice, practice

Meaningful relationships are built on a foundation of effective communication, which includes listening. Fortunately, for anyone interested in practicing effective listening skills, our relationships give us a multitude of opportunities to practice. Commit to becoming an active listener. You have the ability to improve your listening skills with each conversation you have. This is not to suggest that being an active listener is easy. It takes practice. Apply the recommendations in this chapter consistently. And when you do, you will see an improvement in your relationships with those you lead.

Commit today to changing your behavior in your next conversation. Begin by concentrating on a single conversation. Who will you choose to dedicate your single focus to? Will it be your spouse or a child? Perhaps your boss or a coworker? Maybe even the volunteers or team members you lead. When you engage in active listening, you will appreciate how quickly you see the positive results of your improved listening skills, and therefore, your effectiveness as a leader.

Take Action

Over the course of the next week, which of the following areas will you concentrate on to improve your listening skills?

___ Seeking to understand (effective listening)

___ Participating (active listening)

___ Keeping an open mind

___ Paying attention

___ Being engaged

___ Not interrupting

___ Listening with your ears and eyes

___ Feeling what others are saying

___ Eliminating distractions during conversations

4

LANGUAGE — LAGNIAPPE LEGACY LOVE LAUGH LEARN LISTEN

"You can have brilliant ideas, but if you can't get them across, your ideas won't get you anywhere."

Lee Iacocca

While the *L* in Listen focuses on your ability to understand those who communicate with you, the *L* in Language represents the words and behaviors you use to communicate with others. Professionals, couples, parents, and leaders spend millions of dollars to master the use of language. Toastmasters International, an organization with locations on four continents, provides training to millions of people on effective presentation skills. The National Speakers Association provides resources, training, and networking opportunities for those who make a living as professional speakers.

And SkillPath provides businesses with professional development training that includes courses on effective communication skills. Still the language of communication has yet to be mastered by new and seasoned leaders, among others.

A leader's communication skills are critical to his or her success; however, this is only one of the tools in a leader's toolkit. I have known several exceptional speakers who could not lead a class of schoolchildren to a Scottsdale ice cream shop on a hot August afternoon. Conversely, I have witnessed a respected high school student rally a team to victory, a concerned mom convince a school board to change testing rules, and a nonprofit board member encourage donors to give double the previous year's contribution, all through the mastery of language.

The language of leadership is so much more than flowery prose delivered by a gifted orator. The language of leadership is a dialogue, not a monologue. Put another way, it takes two.

Every year, hundreds of books and articles are written on the subject of leadership communication. They have titles that relate to public speaking, effective communication, and how to persuade others. In each of these works, the authors are really addressing the language of leadership.

The words

Many people associate leadership with the ability to communicate with and motivate others using appropriate language. The most basic input of language is the words. Each day, as a leader, you will have multiple interactions that will influence others. What message are the words you speak sending to those around you? This is about perception, the perception of the listener or observer. People often perceive your words differently than the way you intend. So as you wield the power of words in your language, be certain to consider how your words are perceived.

Using inclusive language is one of the most effective forms of communication for leaders. As a leader, you might have the opportunity to speak about team objectives, your department's mission, or your entire company's vision. As a leader in the public sector, you may have to address certain issues that impact the entire community. The language you use in these interactions must go beyond you as the leader and include the interests and concerns of those who are listening: your team, volunteers, donors, constituents, or other stakeholders. In one-on-one sessions or in group meetings that you lead, do people walk away with a feeling of "we're all in this together"?

> "The difference between the right word and the almost right word is the difference between lightning and the lightning bug."
>
> Mark Twain

Here are some examples of inclusive language.

We versus I. When discussing a team's objectives, it is critical that a leader always use the word "we." We denotes teamwork. We infers shared responsibility. We means all of us—together.

Our versus My. Similar to above, the word "our" is also intended to convey unification. As a leader, terms such as "my objectives" or "my goals" should never be used when communicating with team members. As a leader, your words should create a sense of team, a spirit of collaboration, support, and community. The term "our performance" means that everyone has a part in an objective or task.

We versus They. I have witnessed, on countless occasions, a manager use the term "they" to describe decision-makers higher in the organization. During the financial crisis, I was in an audience being addressed by a regional vice president of one of the "Big Three" automobile manufacturers. This regional leader used the term "they" forty-seven times to describe senior leadership in Detroit. Most of the references were associated with negative messages being delivered. Most of the businesspeople in that room worked for the same company, but the language used clearly led to a "we vs. they" or "us vs. them" type of relationship. It appeared that the speaker was attempting to separate himself from the decisions of the senior leadership and gain empathy from others in the company.

There are exceptions to the above. The exception occurs when you're communicating your own mistakes or failures. The words "I" and "my" are appropriate when a leader is referring to his or her own missteps. As a leader, I've used the phrase "I really screwed this one up" on more than one occasion. In addition to the exception of admitting a mistake, it's also appropriate for an effective leader to use the term "I" when referring to praise or gratitude. When statements such as "I have never been more proud" or "I am completely supportive of the decisions you have made" are used by a leader, they are always well received.

Conversely, there are some words that leaders should use daily. To get a handle on these words, consider the most basic etiquette your grandmother taught you.

Do you use kind language? When you commit to using the following phrases on a daily basis, you will notice a change in the way your team responds to you.

Language

Thank you. As a leader, you don't get a free pass on respectful behavior. In fact, it should be a value that you strive to display on a daily basis. Team members perform certain tasks requested by leadership hundreds of times a day. A simple "thank you" goes a long way.

In 1994, I had the opportunity to work with my second personal assistant. When my P.A., Susan, asked on the first day, "How do you take your coffee?" I simply responded, "Cream and sugar," and then thought nothing of the exchange. The next morning, after I sat at my desk, Susan walked into my office with a hot cup of coffee with cream and sugar, and I said, "Wow, thank you." Her face lit up, and she replied with a big smile, "You're welcome. My old boss sat in that chair for ten years and never once said thank you." She was a little more surprised when I explained that if I wanted coffee, I would get a cup, and I'd ask if she needed one as well. I explained that if she was going to get coffee for herself and asked if I wanted one, I thought that would be nice. The words "thank you" are incredibly powerful. So simple, yet used so infrequently.

Please. The word "please" seems to have exited the vocabulary of many leaders. I don't suggest that you end every single request with the word, but I encourage you, as a leader, to say and write the word on a daily basis. Every leader I speak with expresses a desire to be respected (not necessarily liked) by his or her team. I've heard several leaders say, "Respect is a non-negotiable." The quickest way to earn the respect of your team is to show them respect. Both "please" and "thank you" quickly put you on that path. Respect is a two-way street.

I made a mistake. Can I have a spoonful of sugar with that sentence, please? That phrase just does not go down easily, does it? I have to confess that, early in my career, this was something I wasn't very good at. After all, if the boss admits that he or she made a mistake, isn't that a sign of weakness? Leaders don't want to show that weakness or admit to failure, do they?

News flash: Your people already know you screwed up. The majority of the time, those around you realize that you made a bad call or chose the wrong strategy before you're willing to admit it to yourself. Admitting the mistake is usually not a revelation, but the act of saying the words out loud is. Admitting you made a mistake is an opportunity to earn the respect of those you lead. This also provides you, as the leader, with the opportunity to role model the behavior you expect from team members. Never be afraid to admit a mistake because, when done early enough in the process, there's time to minimize the impact. In fact, you can actually turn this humble, honest admission into a reason for your team to view you as a role model.

What do you think? The higher you find your name on an organization chart, the more insulated you become from the people who do the work. One of the risks of being in a leadership role is that people often tell you what they think you want to hear, not necessarily what you need to hear.

"What do you think?" is a question you should ask on a regular basis of people throughout your organization. For those who make decisions based more on emotions than facts, the question is slightly modified: "How do you feel about this?" Either of the alternatives displays that you want your team's input and that you are looking for other opinions. Many times you will receive an answer that's simply the "company line" or the safe reply, to which you reply, "Why do you think or feel that way?" Don't let them off the hook so easily. Again, some people are uncomfortable and even afraid to tell the leader what they really think or feel. So cut your team some slack.

The more often you ask this question, the more likely you are to eventually get an honest reply, and that serves you, as the leader, as well as the entire team. Jack Welch, the revered former CEO of General Electric, once said, "I have lots of people giving me answers; what I need are leaders that ask the right questions." I've always thought this was a provocative statement, as we all know leaders are supposed to have all the answers. Right? No one has all the right answers, but today's great leaders continue to ask lots of questions. What do you think?

Nice job! I am shocked when I read articles or the results of surveys that indicate how infrequently workers in America hear that they've done a good job. For employees who have a high need for words of affirmation to feel engaged, this lack of recognition leads to low morale and lower productivity. We all want to know that we are doing a good job and that we're appreciated for our contributions.

As a leader, find opportunities to notice and recognize great work and great people. The more you recognize exceptional performance, the more exceptional performance you will get. There is a warning here. You have to recognize *great* performance, not simply performance. If you only recognize performance in an attempt to constantly provide positive feedback, the impact of your words will quickly dissipate. In other words, insincere feedback becomes meaningless.

We can do this! Maybe you're thinking, "Okay, Tony Robbins, I already know about the power of positive thinking!" Excuse me as I step down off the soapbox. I do enjoy a lot of Tony's work, and it is testimony to the power of positivity!

In your role as a leader, your team wants you to have a positive attitude. In fact, they *need* you to have a positive attitude. When the odds are against you, and things really look bad, those who follow you take their cues from you. They're not only watching your behavior during difficult times, they're listening to your words. The language you choose is imperative in holding the team together when it seems that everything is falling apart.

In the morning, while team members share coffee, or when they're at lunch, they have conversations about what the boss thinks about this or that. When they know what you think based on the words you've used in their presence, they're likely to discuss that during their "water cooler" moments. Your "can do" spirit goes a long way, far beyond the moment you spoke the words. There is power in a positive attitude. When faced with a tough assignment or in the face of an apparent loss, remember: "We can do this!"

How can I help? This is a great question to ask your team members when there is a difficult task or issue facing them. It's best to pose the question after you've had an opportunity to thoroughly discuss the issue or problem. This question displays your own engagement and a willingness to assist a team member during a tough time. Of course, many times your team members will say, "I have this," and your involvement won't be necessary. But on those occasions when your input or assistance can make a difference, the fact that you are willing to help will demonstrate to others that you are part of the team.

The written word

In a digital world, so much of our communication is through email and text messages that both rising leaders and seasoned veterans need a keen awareness of the messages being sent in cyberspace.

Even with the billions of electronic messages sent every year, the actual written word (by hand, on paper) still provides meaningful impact to the recipient. For both forms of written communication, hard copy as well as digital, you must be careful in crafting your messages. As a leader, your spoken message is processed through multiple lenses: verbal (words), vocal (tone), and visual (body language). In written format, as the sender of the message, you don't have the luxury of fully communicating tone and body language. Although the receiver will interpret the tone of the message on his own, as the leader, you must rely solely on the words to accurately communicate your intention.

Here is one very common example of how tone can be communicated in the written word. I'm sure you're familiar with this approach, as it has been seen far too many times. As a leader, you should avoid this at all costs. Trust me, there's a better way.

I WANT THIS REPORT RIGHT NOW!!!!!!!

Bold capital letters followed by exclamation points leave little doubt about the tone of this communication. The language seems clear, and the intention of the request seems plainly stated. The sender is apparently in urgent need of this report and seems to be screaming at the recipient. Notice that I have said "apparently" and "seems" in the above observation. With only the written word on which to base one's opinion, the recipient could assume "right now" means this very second and that he should stop everything to hand-deliver the report. However, this message could mean that the sender needs the report in the next few hours or by the end of the day.

There are two critical points to be made from this example. First, when communicating in written form, be aware that the tone of your message is an important component. Do all you can to communicate your intended tone so your recipient doesn't have to guess. In this instance, the recipient is basing his interpretation of tone not on the sender's voice inflections, but rather on the sender's choice of punctuation, use of all caps, word selection, and length of communication. If you send all your correspondence with all caps and bold letters to indicate urgency, the urgency of the message becomes even more unclear. If everything you send is urgent, then nothing is really urgent.

With regard to digital forms of communication, I have been accused of being in a bad mood when responding to an email with the single word "No." Oftentimes, however, I might be boarding a flight or in the midst of some other consuming activity that doesn't allow me to reply in greater length. This leaves the recipient of my reply to interpret my tone as curt or angry when, in fact, that isn't my intention. So is it the recipient's responsibility to get over it, or is it my responsibility as a leader to use words more effectively? I have come to realize that adding two simple words to this short reply can smooth things over. Instead, I reply, "No, thank you." Easy and done. The difference is indeed subtle, but impactful.

Clarity is critical

For some, email has become an effective, and even essential, form of communication. But the clarity of your message can be easily lost in email. Therefore, when choosing to use email or text messaging, ensure that your language is clear and concise. Read it multiple times before sending. If the communication is critical or urgent, always follow up with a phone call or face-to-face conversation to validate your intent.

During a meeting with one of our vice presidents, this subject came up as part of the feedback he received in an evaluation. Team members suggested that he work on the clarity of requests he made of them. A simple question could have a profound effect on this communication. "To make sure we are both on the same page, can you briefly describe what we just agreed on?" This could be the steps of a project, a deadline, or a strategy. At the end of a meeting, simply ask for clarity on what was said or agreed upon. When both parties walk away from a meeting with a common understanding of deliverables and responsibilities, the opportunity for future problems is significantly reduced.

Download my Clarity Checklist at www.MikePitcher.net to help ensure your digital communications are as effective as they can be.

Reply all

If I had the opportunity to meet the team that created email, I would have one very serious recommendation for them: eliminate the "reply all" response option. If told by the extremely rich computer wizard that this was an impossible request, I would simply suggest the following pop up after hitting the "reply all" option: Are you absolutely, positively sure you want to make a jackass of yourself in front of all of the people you just copied on this response? Are you really sure?

I do not know a single person in a leadership role who hasn't regretted, at least one time, hitting the dreaded "reply all" key. When you are angry, frustrated, under immense pressure, and especially if you've had a libation or two, think long and hard about the "reply all" option. Like words of anger that leave your lips, you can't take these emails back. And yes, this comes from personal experience. One other bit of sage advice. If you do chose to reply to all or you choose to forward, make darn sure you've read the entire email thread all the way to the bottom. I'm just saying.

I earlier referenced the brilliant technologists that created email. It's worth noting that Google recently introduced a recall feature in the Google Mail application. There are some very smart people working for this Mountain View-based juggernaut.

The spoken word

The ability to stand in front of an audience and clearly articulate your vision or objective with passion and commitment is a skill that all leaders should possess. However, you don't have to be exceptional, you simply have to be effective.

It has been noted that the myth of executive communication is that it ever happened in the first place. Most business executives think they're adequately equipped to communicate with their teams; however, most of their employees probably don't share this opinion, and there have been several research projects that indicate this to be true.

In their book, *The Leader's Voice*, authors Boyd Clarke and Ron Crossland offer results of a study on the effectiveness of executive communication. The researchers asked executives from America's largest companies to rate their own level of effectiveness when communicating with employees. These executives scored themselves as either "very effective" (47%) or "somewhat effective" (46%), for a total of 93 percent in the top two categories. In other words, a little more than 9 out of 10 executives believed they were at least minimally effective when communicating to their employees. The researchers then interviewed frontline managers and supervisors of the same companies and determined that 29 percent of employees felt senior executives were either effective or somewhat effective, leaving 71 percent with the view that executive communication was either "not too effective" or "not effective at all."[12]

For communication to be effective, it must be so for the individual who receives the message. Leaders must continually solicit feedback to ensure that the desired message was first received and then understood. Clarity is critical!

For 99 percent of leaders, using the spoken word to communicate occurs naturally each day in meetings, in hallway conversations, and in problem-solving discussions with team members. On the surface, this type of communication may seem rather mundane and routine, but the astute leader understands that these interactions form the foundation of how he or she is perceived as a leader. In fact, academics have recently named "conversational leadership" as an important part of every leader's daily activities. The words you speak, your tone of voice, and your body language are all elements that define you, not only in that meeting, but for weeks or months afterward. As a leader, what you say counts! As a leader, what you say matters!

At LeasePlan, there's a software developer named Bob. (I'll disclose his full name shortly.) Bob was hired to develop dashboard reporting for our clients so that when users log into our system, they can immediately see KPIs (key performance indicators) on a customized dashboard on their computer screen. During a meeting with our executive team, our CIO demonstrated the new dashboard technology that Bob had developed. The entire team was extremely impressed with the look and feel of the software and the apparent ease of use. By the way, Bob wasn't in the room. I share this fact because if he were, I would probably not have asked the

---

12 Boyd Clarke and Rod Crossland, The Leader's Voice: How Your Communication Can Inspire Action and Get Results! (New York: Select Books, 2002), 24.

following question: "I love the new dashboards! Did Ponytail Bob create this?"

There are a lot of men named Bob who work at LeasePlan. At the time of this meeting, I didn't know this Bob's last name. I did know that he wears his hair in a ponytail. The comment seemed harmless and natural to me, so I described our new employee as "Ponytail Bob." Our CIO responded that it was indeed our new team member who designed the new dashboard. I left the meeting feeling great about our new technology for our clients.

Imagine my surprise, and my embarrassment, when several weeks later, during a discussion with members of our operations team, someone referred to the new guy in IT as, you guessed it, Ponytail Bob. In a private meeting, I apologized to Mr. Bob Pearson for this faux pas. After almost a year of regretting what I had started, I decided to apologize in a town hall setting in front of the entire company. When I did, I shook Bob's hand, and he actually laughed it off, and said, "Let's talk later." In a one-on-one discussion, Bob laughed and said, "You really don't have to sweat this Ponytail Bob thing!" He also explained that his personal website was now named Ponytail Bob, his homemade wine was labeled Ponytail Bob, and his close friends now called him "PTB." I literally laughed out loud when Bob said, "I actually want to thank you for creating my brand!"

Thankfully, this incident worked out very well. I can give you countless examples of comments I've made that did not result in happy endings. My point is your words matter. People are always listening to what you say. "I didn't really mean it" is an excuse that doesn't work in leadership.

Public speaking

It has been said that public speaking is the number one fear of most people. For many leaders, speaking before an audience is an activity that raises the blood pressure and tests the chemical efficiency of their deodorant.

I have been blessed with the opportunity to address audiences ranging from twenty to two thousand. Although I'm very comfortable in these settings, I must confess that, on many occasions, I get nervous prior to the beginning of a presentation. Almost everyone experiences a little anxiety prior to speaking in front of an audience. The key to success is to use the adrenaline rush in a positive way. It's important to remember that the rush you feel is a normal reaction to this situation. Your response to that adrenaline rush should be fueled by your self-confidence.

Confidence is the by-product of proper preparation, and confidence is at the foundation of every great presentation. If speaking to large groups is part of your job description, there are several great books on the subject and coaches who would be willing to help enhance your speaking skills. However, if you present to large groups less frequently, here are a few suggestions to improve your performance.

Know your subject. This seems ridiculously obvious, but I have seen far too many presentations where the presenter was unsure of the facts. Generally, if you're presenting, you are viewed as the expert in the room (not necessarily to be mistaken with "smartest person in the room"). Ensure that you're well-versed in the subject matter, that you have command of certain facts and data, and that your information is correct. In this age of instant information, don't be surprised when people instantly refer to Google to validate information that you present. Several excellent presentations have been completely derailed by an audience member who used a smartphone to find information contrary to the information being presented. Not only does this usually turn into an unnecessary debate, but as a presenter, your credibility is questioned.

Practice. Ample practice is important when speaking to a large audience, but just as important when presenting to a team of ten in a business setting or when speaking to fifteen members of your Sunday School class. Find time in your schedule to practice key points of your presentation. If you have practiced a presentation ten or twenty times, the words will come naturally when it's show time.

Nail the beginning and the end. Our vice president of sales condenses the entire presentation process into a simple formula: tell them what you are going to tell them; tell them; and tell them what you told them. I believe in the simplicity, and therefore recommend that you have the two bookends of the process completely nailed down. I don't suggest you memorize the beginning and ending of your presentation word for word; however, be certain you can easily recite the first and last thirty to forty-five seconds. Your confidence level (and therefore your performance level) will dramatically increase.

Practice the beginning and the closing as separate sections, and once you have mastered each, the middle section (the tell 'em part) will come naturally. As you prepare for your presentation, write down the first four to five sentences and perfect each sentence on paper. Practice your opening and closing to a point where, if you were awakened in the middle of the night, you could sit up and deliver the words as if you were on stage. The confidence you gain by owning these two parts of any presentation will give you an amazing level of confidence about your ability to perform, which in turn ensures success when the time comes for the actual event.

Use humor (with care). Remember Chapter 1: Laugh? There is great power in humor, and laughter makes people feel good. To use humor in a speech or a presentation is always a good choice—if you're funny! If you choose to insert humor into any presentation, get a second opinion on the content. Many presentations have been completely derailed by the joke that fell flat and the ensuing beads of sweat that rolled down the presenter's forehead. If you're not absolutely certain the material is funny, don't use it.

Early in my career, when my daughters were much younger, I would practice short presentations with them. You'll be surprised by the valuable feedback you can receive from family members. On one occasion, my daughter Michelle warned me that a joke I was going to tell at the beginning of my presentation wasn't funny. I used the line anyway. It fell completely flat, and then I struggled through the rest of the speech, wishing I had listened to my young advisor.

Your audience does not know when you make a mistake. In general, unless you're in a business setting and use the wrong data, the audience has no idea when you make a mistake. If you forget a section, or you seem to stumble through one part, no one really knows. Relax. You know that you were supposed to provide a certain example to emphasize a point, but you move to the next subject without the reference. If you carry on flawlessly without drawing attention to your misstep, your audience is none the wiser.

Don't be tempted to apologize for something during your presentation, as the audience doesn't know about your faux pas unless you tell them. I rarely provide advice that starts with the word "never," but *never* begin a presentation or speech by apologizing for the fact that you're not a good public speaker.

Lowering your audience's expectations with your opening sentence won't win you sympathy, but will simply disconnect many people from the very beginning.

Have a conversation. The most effective speakers and presenters I have seen make the interaction with the audience seem like a personal conversation. I've been in a large audience when the speaker was on top of his or her game, and I felt like they were speaking directly to me. When questions were asked, I answered each in my head as if the speaker read my thoughts, and with a smile or nod, the speaker seemed to acknowledge my response.

Regardless of the size of the room, make direct eye contact with members of the audience. If you're presenting to five people at a table or five hundred in an auditorium, make direct eye contact with some of the individuals in the room. All you have to do is hold that eye contact for a few seconds, and this will establish a connection with you and audience members. If you smile when appropriate, they will smile back. In a large setting, look both right and left to find audience members who are looking back at you. Although this will seem mechanical at first, with practice it will appear that you are simply having a conversation with the entire room.

Become a storyteller. This concept is meaningful for both your presentations and your personal interactions. Rarely do those around you remember facts and figures, but everyone remembers stories. The New Testament of the Bible, one of the most widely read books in history, is a collection of stories about Jesus and how he interacted with others. People remember stories. There are stories in your business, in your family, and among your friends that are meaningful and impactful. These stories are the threads that weave a mosaic of who you are and what you believe in. Your audience will remember the stories you told and associate your message with the story.

Scholars have argued that Dr. Martin Luther King Jr.'s "I Have a Dream" speech, delivered in Washington, DC, in 1963, was the speech with the greatest impact of the 20th century. Dr. King's speech is an amazing example of painting pictures with words. It is difficult, even when simply reading the text rather than hearing the emotion in King's voice, to not be moved by the message in his words.

In every sentence and every reference, King's passion and emotion come through. He tells of an America that is not ideal and then shares his vision for what this country could be if the promises made to all were actually fulfilled. He uses the geography and the landscape of America as a canvas to illustrate the vast diversity that surrounds and influences its people. And he brings to light, with respectful, nonthreatening, yet determined language, the fact that unless a change is made voluntarily, a change will surely be made forcefully.

As a guest lecturer at Emory University and the University of Georgia, I always ask a class if they have read the entire speech. Surprisingly, only about a third of students raise their hands. I share this speech with my classes, not because the students will necessarily go on to make speeches that have global impact, but in hopes that their presentations will have immediate impact on those they lead.

Search online to read the full text of King's speech and watch or listen to his historic presentation. His cadence and tone have tremendous impact on the audience. Pay close attention to the imagery he uses as he attempts to reach out to those who live in every corner of the United States. Like Dr. Martin Luther King Jr., you should use the language of inclusion when communicating.

Use words that are a call to action. Become a great storyteller. If you influence always, you should always be a positive influence.

Okay to Q and A (on your terms). As a speaker, on many occasions you will be asked to do a Q and A (question and answer) session. This is an excellent opportunity for you to provide further information and additional details on your presentation. Obviously, you will need to be prepared for this type of session. I am a firm believer, however, that you should position the Q and A prior to *your* closing statements (or even better, your closing story). If your presentation is thirty minutes or longer, a standard question session would be ten to fifteen minutes. Earlier in this chapter, I suggested that you nail your opening and your closing statements. This requires that you don't allow someone in the audience to close your presentation with a question. When appropriate, simply say, "We have time for one more question." After you've answered the last question, transition to your closing message or story.

I also recommend that you have one question in mind that you can ask just in case no one raises their hand with a question from the audience. Generally, this gives the audience time to think of additional questions. If I've been asked to facilitate a Q and A on this material, and no one raises their hand, I may ask, "What makes people more afraid of speaking in public than of dying?"

Body language

One of the most overlooked influences of successful communication is the body language of a leader. This unspoken form of communication has significant impact on how you're viewed as a leader. What does your body language say about you? Some leaders are described as having presence when they enter a room. As impressive as that may be, I believe that no one is born with this mystical presence. This is a skill that an astute man or woman has worked to develop. If you enter a room with your shoulders held back, and your head held high, smiling at those who engage in eye contact, you will notice a difference in the way people greet you. Your body language should make the statement that you want to be in this situation and that you have a purpose. People will notice.

This skill takes practice. This concept is certainly not limited to a business setting. As a leader, how do you enter your workplace every day? As an educator, what does your body language tell your students at the beginning of every class? As an athlete, what message are you sending your teammates and your competitors when you get on the court or the field of play?

Recently, professional athletes have come under fire for inappropriate body language. Jay Cutler, a quarterback in the NFL with the Chicago Bears, has been admonished in the media for his body language on the sidelines. Cutler will sit on a bench alone, away from other teammates, and stare into the heavens or simply stare at the grass, usually after a mistake on the field. Simply put, Cutler's body language sends the wrong message for a quarterback, a perceived leader on and off the field. Even Congressional leaders have been questioned about their body language during sessions in both the House and the Senate. In an era of constant media coverage, it seems that someone is always watching. Remember that even if your lips aren't moving, your body language is still communicating.

Your facial expressions, in particular, serve as a billboard when you communicate. When you talk to your team members, family members, and others, consider the non-verbal cues you send. Here are a few to practice:

- Look others directly in the eyes when talking to them and listening to them.
- Nod during a discussion.
- Stand and sit upright, not slouched.
- In front of a group, widen your stance, and use open arm gestures.
- Vary your facial expressions in response to the conversation (raise eyebrows, smile, etc.).
- Smile authentically, but avoid laughing inappropriately with a big grin.
- Avoid being distracted by a clock, a watch, other people, or your own digital devices when others are speaking to you.

If before now, you haven't been aware of what your body language is communicating about your leadership style, from here on out, pay attention. With regard to the last bullet, I once interviewed a candidate for a senior level sales position who continually looked at his watch. Twice during the interview, he actually looked at his cell phone. I asked if everything was all right, as I was concerned it could be a personal issue. He replied that everything was fine, and upon his next time check, I concluded the interview. His body language communicated the message that there was something more important than this career opportunity. Remember your body is communicating even when your mouth is not moving.

As you mature on your leadership journey, and even if you have been in a leadership role for decades, I encourage you to peruse a bookstore or search the Internet, as you will find several works dedicated to the subject of language in communication. On this single topic, a search of related book titles on Amazon produces more than 23,000 results. That is a lot of advice on language and communication skills. The time you invest in developing this critical skill will pay impressive dividends.

Take Action

How will you change your communication in each of the areas below?

The Words _____

The Written Word _____

The Spoken Word _____

Body Language _____

5

LAUGH · LEARN · LISTEN · LANGUAGE · LAGNIAPPE · LEGACY · LOVE

> *"It's the little things that a leader does that can make a big difference to those they are fortunate enough to lead."*
>
> Mike Pitcher

Lagniappe. What a strange word. What does it mean? Pronounced "lan-yap," this word has its origin in my birthplace, Louisiana. It means "a little something extra!" That's what great leaders do. Great leaders do the little things that others don't do. Many know lagniappe by another term, "a baker's dozen," a term made popular when people shopped at the local bakery and the baker would put thirteen items in the bag, instead of twelve. Because of that "little extra," most people went back to that same bakery time and again. From athletics, to personal relationships, to career, most people can name those who have provided a little lagniappe.

Lagniappe is something that sets people apart.

Michael O'Connell: A lesson in lagniappe

In 1980, I began my professional career as a postage meter salesman with Pitney Bowes. In 1980, Pitney Bowes was one of the "Big Three" firms in the office equipment industry, with the other two being IBM and Xerox (yes, times have changed). Back then, these firms rarely hired a recent college graduate to represent them in sales. The trend at the time was to find sales professionals who had five to ten years of selling experience and a proven track record of success. I was thrilled to land a job at a Fortune 300 company, and I busted my butt to ensure my boss would never feel disappointed for taking a chance on a young college graduate with little sales experience.

Three years after joining the company, and after building a record of exceeding sales quotas, I was promoted to the position of Sales Team Manager (STM). In January of 1984, I was the youngest STM in the company, and I had the privilege of leading my first sales team in Lafayette, Louisiana. I hardly knew what I was doing in those days, but I was blessed with exceptional mentors—Campbell, Graham, and Nabors—who helped me understand the art and science of sales management. The learning process was similar to taking a drink of water from a fire hose. It was difficult to do, but once you got a taste, it was fulfilling.

For decades, Pitney Bowes held town hall gatherings, called the Annual Job Holders Meeting, in each of the company's one hundred districts. A panel comprised of local management, regional management, and one senior executive from corporate headquarters fielded questions from employees. If a question could not be answered during the meeting, a written response was promised within sixty days. The practice of giving every employee a direct line to senior management was one of the practices that earned Pitney Bowes a spot in Jim Collins's best-selling book *From Good to Great.*

During this time, the senior vice president responsible for the entire field sales organization (in 1984, PB had over 2,400 field sales professionals) was Mike O'Connell. Mike was a brawny Irish Catholic guy who looked like an offensive lineman. He was gifted with a booming voice, once described as sounding like "the voice of God." Everyone loved Mike O'Connell, but all knew that, when it came to selling and sales, he was a driven and tough vice president. He was also known as a man with a big heart. Mike was known for remembering many of his employees' names and small details about a person that seemed impossible to remember for a man in his position. He was loved by so many people, and when Mike needed to hit a sales number, the troops were ready to make the calls necessary for us to make him proud; we owed it to Mike.

Imagine my surprise when I was told by my branch manager that I was assigned to drive Michael O'Connell from the Job Holders Meeting in Baton Rouge to the next meeting in New Orleans. I was scared to death. What if I got into a wreck? What if I got lost? The drive was ninety minutes down one interstate, with only two turns, but that didn't matter. What if I said something really stupid? I was known for being a bit of a cowboy.

After the Baton Rouge meeting, Mike O'Connell and I hit the road. We chatted about the company and college football for the first thirty minutes. Then, Mike pulled out a large stack of Polaroid pictures. (A "Polaroid" was a physical photograph produced immediately by a special Polaroid camera.) He viewed the front of the first picture, flipped it over, and then read the writing on the back:

"Phil Thibodeaux, ten years this year with Pitney." He spent the rest of the drive with the deck of photographs, memorizing the information on the back, which included names of children, recent births, anniversaries, or outstanding sales results. I was amazed at his ability to look at the information once or twice and commit it to memory. As I pulled up to the hotel and put the car in park, Mike put his big left paw on my shoulder and said, "Now, this is our little secret, right, Pitch?" Then he winked at me. I have never told this story until now. It is one of my favorite examples of lagniappe.

Mike O'Connell passed away several years ago, tragically only a few years after retiring. I am confident that he would smile at me for sharing this story. He always seemed to do a little extra.

For decades he made a great deal of money and earned thousands of shares of stock options, yet he spent endless hours studying the names and faces of his team members. Mike did this so that when he walked into an office he could genuinely speak with team members about their family and personal lives. People knew he was a leader with a heart; they knew he cared. He gave a little extra. He did more than what was expected. To those who worked with Mike, he was a legendary leader. He sincerely cared about the well-being of those he was responsible for leading. This is a real-life example of lagniappe. It's also an example of what others remember when they have the opportunity to encounter a great leader.

I have often wondered how many sales managers drove Mike from one city to the next and watched this little ritual. Not one of them ever spoke about this practice of his. No one ever tried to minimize the effort by suggesting he really doesn't remember thousands of names and he just studied the night before. What it boiled down to is that Mike O'Connell made the effort and proved that he cared enough to do the little things that other people in his position didn't do. He took the time to remember people's names as well as spending time talking about more than just business results.

Remember names

Each year at LeasePlan, we survey our entire staff to determine how team members feel about working at the company. I am surprised (and pleased) that one point that continues to be mentioned is that I know almost everyone's name. Our team members take great pride in this fact. I work under the premise that they know my name, so I should know theirs. Perhaps if I was the CEO of Microsoft, this would be a real problem.

Many people say to themselves, "I'm not good at remembering names." As Henry Ford said, "If you think you can, or you think you can't, you're right!" This skill comes with practice, and focused leaders can get really good at it by concentrating on the process. I won't document the science of remembering names or suggest the dozens of memory techniques practiced, but I believe you can do this when you choose to. I will offer you one key to remembering names that will change how you think about it. Start saying to yourself, "I am good at remembering people's names!" Then, start doing it. One more time for dramatic emphasis. Constantly say to yourself, "I am good at remembering people's names." Trust me on this one; it works. I will share with you the technique that I've found most successful, and it's based on the theory of repetition.

When you meet someone, remember to continuously use his or her name during the conversation. An example of this practice is upon first introduction. As soon as you're introduced, use the person's name. Instead of saying, "It's nice to meet you," choose to say, "Sharon, it's great to meet you." During the course of the conversation, instead of saying, "I thought that movie was absolutely hysterical," you could say, "Sharon, that movie was absolutely hysterical." While an incredibly subtle difference, the use of the person's name in your dialogue helps to cement the name in your memory. Recall will occur easily on your next meeting. And what if it doesn't? What if you don't remember Sharon's name next time? Be bold, be different, and do the little things that others don't. Simply say, "I apologize, and I'm really sorry that I don't remember your name. Help me." When she does, respond, "Sharon, thank you. I'm so sorry for not remembering." And once you have done this, you won't forget her name the next time.

Celebrate the little victories

One of the easiest ways to practice the eLement of lagniappe is to celebrate the little victories. Every leader celebrates landing the largest deal in company history. Every coach celebrates a team's championship win. And of course, every dad celebrates when his child earns a college scholarship. Some parents might even get flagged for excessive celebration. (Pardon the football metaphor. It's just part of my DNA.) Any of the aforementioned events can and should trigger significant recognition and celebratory activities, but what about the student who skips attending the Friday night football game to study for the Monday morning calculus test? How about the celebration of the extraordinary practice that the team gives after a loss the week before? Shouldn't these small victories also qualify for celebration?

The human spirit longs to be recognized for doing something good. In many cases, the recognition is more important than the good deed. I've defined leadership as influence. As a leader, you always influence those around you. This concept is evident in one of the most challenging leadership roles of all, that of a parent.

For children, positive reinforcement helps build character and confidence. Celebrating the little victories—from learning to ride a bike to tying a shoe or writing his or her name—makes a child want to do more, to try harder. Recognition of the little wins, accompanied by the feeling of accomplishment, is the fuel that ignites the desire for greater achievement. As a parent, how can you continue to reward and recognize the little victories that happen every week? First, you have to watch for them. Then, you have to celebrate them. Does this mean a drive to get ice cream? Does it mean popping an Apple iTunes card in a lunchbox? Is the reward dinner at your son's favorite all-you-can-eat restaurant with a couple of his friends? It's possible that the reward is less important than the fact that you recognize the effort, the little victories.

> The human spirit longs to be recognized for doing something good.

Using examples of leadership that include parenting, athletics, and most often, the business arena might seem strange to some. But your leadership style and behavior rarely change based on the setting. You interact with people in a consistent manor. The dad who coaches Little League and concentrates on development and making the game fun tends to do the same with his team at work. The daughter who remembers birthdays and special occasions for her family tends to do the same with team members at work. Unfortunately, the same dad who yells and screams at his children for missteps at home tends to behave the same at work as someone's boss.

A great deal of research has been done on the topic of rewarding achievement in the business environment. A statistic I find alarming is that half of American workers have not been told in the last six months that they're doing a good job. This statistic is tragic. If the subset was the U.S. Congress, okay, I get it, but not for the average worker. How can this be? All it takes is for leaders to first be aware when something good occurs and then to recognize it. Someone sold something. Someone fixed something. Someone found something. Someone helped someone. Someone solved a problem. Someone wrote something. Someone eliminated something. Someone invented something. You get the picture. Every day, every hour, someone you lead does something that could be considered a small victory. *Celebrate it!*

You'd be amazed that, as you celebrate the little wins and incremental improvements, larger victories will follow. So what are some of the little victories you could celebrate as a leader?

Celebrate this:
- Your child earned a great test score.
- Your son studied for hours for a test.
- Your daughter volunteered for a charity event.
- Your daughter made a team.
- A customer complaint was handled.
- A proposal was submitted on time.
- Someone got the appointment.
- The doctor said, "Negative."
- The doctor said, "Positive."
- The engine started when you turned the key.
- A new software version was successful.

- You're four pounds down.
- We turned it in on time.
- We made a profit.
- We cooked a great dinner.
- You finished the race.

Every day, opportunities are presented for you to celebrate the little win. Do it! Why is this lagniappe? It's lagniappe because it's a little something extra. It's lagniappe because the celebration is something most people don't take the time to do. Begin to sharpen your awareness of the little victories around you, and take the time to celebrate them.

Handwritten notes

I'm aware that I could be treading on the grounds of generational differences with this one. I am a baby boomer—fifty-seven at the time of this writing—and there could be a difference of opinion on the value of the handwritten word. However, based on what I've experienced with the members of both Gen X and Gen Y, I'm confident that the handwritten note or letter still packs a significant punch. Why? Because in a digital world, it is simply something that most people don't do. Today, we email, we Facebook, we Snapchat, and we text. Guess what? So does everyone else. The handwritten letter or note is different. Today, these communication techniques are rarely used, and yes, each is remembered.

I write a minimum of three notes each week to recognize something someone has done. I look for triggers to acknowledge a behavior or a success that can best be expressed in a personal, handwritten note. In the business world, examples of triggers include closing a sale, gaining a new client, or learning a new skill. At our company, we introduced a new development program, and each of our employees received a journal to document their progress. I wrote a personal note on the inside cover of every journal. Many people thought it was a printed stamp until they compared notes and realized that each one included a slightly different message. Although it took a little extra time to finish this project, team members reacted to this act of lagniappe by taking the training seriously.

To help make the process of creating handwritten notes even more personal:

- Purchase nice stationery that you would consider unique.
- Use your favorite pen.
- Handwrite the address on the envelope.
- Take the time to ensure your message is well thought out. Try not to use a generic comment, such as "You did a great job, thanks." (As this alone could be considered insincere.) The notes that I receive and remember (many in digital form, and that's okay by me) are sincere and heartfelt.
- If possible, send a few via the postal service. (People still get excited when opening an unexpected card found in the mailbox.)

People cherish handwritten notes. When I walk the floors of our offices, I often see a notecard that I've sent tacked on a team member's cubicle or attached to the office wall of a manager. My children still enjoy receiving notes and cards from me in the mail. If you're not yet convinced that this bit of lagniappe is a necessary eLement of leadership, my request is to simply try it. Start slowly and see what happens. Begin with the goal of writing one note per week. It can be to a coworker, a relative, or your spouse. Make the commitment to continue the practice for a few months, and notice the difference it makes in the quality of your relationships. I promise you that it will. Why? Because there aren't a lot of people who do it.

Some ideal situations for handwritten messages:
- To your spouse, saying thank you for something special
- To a coworker for helping you with a project
- To your child (in a lunchbox) that simply says "I'm proud of you"
- To a client, thanking them for seeing you on such short notice
- To your child's teacher for helping explain a complex problem
- To your boss, saying thanks for recognizing your efforts on a project
- To thank your assistant for saving your butt by getting the aforementioned project to your boss on time
- To your mom to say thank you for any one of the million things moms do for us
- To your father to thank him for all he has done to shape the person you are (remember this one, as I'll come back to it in a later chapter)

Take a walk

When was the last time you took a walk? I don't mean for exercise, although that's certainly a necessary step in the right direction. I mean taking a walk around your office, locker room, neighborhood, or wherever those you want to meet congregate. As a leader, you need to walk around. Wander into each department and meet the people in your workplace. Get to know your team members and learn about what's happening on the front lines of your organization.

A few years ago, I read a story about a Fortune 500 CEO who had an express elevator installed in the company's headquarters so he wouldn't have to stop on other floors on his way to the top. He missed a great opportunity to spend time every day with the people he led, discover what was important to them, and gain valuable insight about his business. In addition, a shared elevator ride would have created an opportunity for him to establish countless new relationships with the people he was fortunate enough to lead. As it turns out (and this is no surprise), this CEO was fired three years later.

Many leaders don't control their own calendars. They have every minute of the day scheduled by someone else (my someone else is my assistant, Peta). If you are blessed (or cursed, depending on your perspective) to have someone manage your schedule, have your assistant schedule blocks of time to take a walk. "Building culture" is a great placeholder on your calendar for a weekly walk around your business.

The same is true for your household (although this interaction should happen daily in this case), your neighborhood, your church or synagogue, and even your club—wherever you seek to show leadership. Make time to meet, interact with, and engage with people. It will do wonders for your disposition and help you gain valuable insight into what matters to people.

Admit your mistakes

Many leaders, particularly men, find admitting mistakes extremely difficult to do. Admitting your mistakes becomes easier with practice, and God knows, we all have lots of opportunities to practice.

Lagniappe

Admitting your mistakes not only helps show your human side to those you lead, it also implies that you're not perfect, nor do you think you are.

Leadership literature refers to this as being authentic. Admitting your mistakes is evidence of your authenticity. Unfortunately, admitting one's own mistakes is very difficult for many leaders to do. In today's fast-paced, rapidly changing world, it's impossible to know everything and be right all the time. So on those occasions when you are wrong, when you make an error, just admit it. Pride, followed by insecurity, is the dominant emotion that prevents this from happening on a regular basis. Interestingly, the majority of your team knows when you're wrong, especially if you lead a high performing group of Type-A personalities. In the end, not admitting your shortcoming does you more harm than good and threatens your credibility among your team. So if most of the people around you already know it, simply admit your mistake.

The words are pretty simple and straightforward. "Team, it looks like I was wrong on this one. I'm sorry." That seems really simple in print, doesn't it? The difficult part is saying the words out loud, but with practice and sincerity it gets easier.

I love what I do for a living. We have a great organization, but I always tell our team that we will never be perfect. There is one primary reason: I'm the CEO. LeasePlan will never be perfect because I am part of our team, and I screw things up on a regular basis (not on purpose, of course). I want the team to be aware that I know I mess things up sometimes, as they have done (and will do) as well. I also want people to know that it's okay to make a mistake. I would rather we try new things on a consistent basis and, when something doesn't work out, just say, "It was a mistake," and move on. Better yet, we can say, "Well, we learned another way that won't work," and then move on.

Random acts of kindness

In a leadership role, you are blessed in countless ways. I'm convinced that giving something back to others, particularly when they don't expect it, is also a gift you give to yourself. Why is this a form of lagniappe? Because it's the little extra effort that most leaders don't do.

During the fourth quarter of 2014, I posted on both Facebook and LinkedIn a challenge for my friends and contacts to do one random act of kindness during the holiday season. I was amazed that the link and the thread took on a life of its own. During a town hall meeting at LeasePlan, I mentioned my personal initiative, and again I was surprised by the response. I began to get emails, voicemails, and texts describing little things that people were doing for others. Examples included reaching across someone's shoulder to pay for their lunch at a fast food restaurant, paying the toll for the car behind you, or simply saying "thank you" to a member of the military that you see in uniform. I later learned that there are websites dedicated to the topic of random acts of kindness.

One week before Christmas, a good Samaritan walked into an Atlanta Walmart and cut in the line at the layaway counter. Much to the joy of those behind this stranger in line, he took out his credit card and paid the remaining balances for those Walmart shoppers. This "secret Santa" disappeared prior to anyone discovering his identity. Those present said he was as happy as any one of his beneficiaries, which was difficult to believe, as many mothers were crying from this incredible random act of kindness. Not all acts of kindness can be as grand as the Walmart secret Santa. However, I find it incredibly gratifying that one little random act of kindness can make someone's day.

I fly several times a month, and since Atlanta's airport is one of the busiest in the world, I always see military personnel in the terminals. On occasion, I have picked up the tab for several of them at a Starbucks or paid their bill at a fast food restaurant. Whenever I see members of our military in a group, I stick my head in and say, "Ladies and gentlemen, thank you for serving." I simply want them to know that their service is truly appreciated.

Once, when traveling with my wife, Sheri, I spotted a large group of soldiers waiting to board a flight. I stuck my head over one of the men's shoulder and told the group thanks, and then I kept walking. After walking about fifty yards down the terminal hallway, a young man about twenty-two years old touched my shoulder. He was accompanied by another soldier, with blonde hair and blue eyes, who looked even younger. The young man with his hand on my arm said, "Sir, not five minutes before you walked up, I was telling my friend about meeting a guy in the Atlanta airport that bought me a coffee and said thanks for serving. And then you showed up—again!" He told me how much it meant to him that someone would show their appreciation. I am still touched by this, and obviously, now I make sure that, whenever I can, I acknowledge our military and say thank you.

Lagniappe is happening all around you

One of the benefits of social media is the ability to reach a large group of people in a short period of time. While working on this chapter, I asked my contacts on both Facebook and LinkedIn about real-world examples of lagniappe. As I had hoped, the practice of lagniappe is alive and well. Even though dozens of my friends and contacts were not familiar with the term, they indeed practiced or they were the beneficiaries of this goodwill. Examples that were submitted included both personal acts and lagniappe provided by a leader of a company or an organization. Some responses were:

- The plumber who comes to your door and then puts cloth covers on his shoes before walking into your home. (Next time, who you gonna call?)
- A fast food restaurant owner who had to close his business for two months to remodel. He paid his hourly staff every week, as if they had worked the entire time.
- A sales manager who, whenever he made a new hire, invited the new employee and their spouse or partner to a dinner. He explained that he knows that it will be a team effort and wants to thank both in advance for their commitment.
- During August in New Orleans, a business provides free snowballs every Friday for every employee. (For those of you not from the Deep South, a snowball is also called a snow cone.)
- An Atlanta business provides between $250 and $1500 holiday bonuses in December. The amount depends on the level of success the business has had that year.
- At the end of a good meal in which the service was exceptional, a friend of mine asks the waiter or waitress what their favorite dessert is at the restaurant, and then she orders that dessert to go. When it's delivered, she gives it back to the server and tells them the dessert is for them to take home.
- In Ohio, a local car club found out about a young boy living with cerebral palsy who loved exotic cars and muscle cars. The group drove dozens of their cars past

the young boy's front porch for his enjoyment, and the last vehicle was his favorite. The driver turned into the delighted youth's driveway and allowed him to sit in the driver's seat.
- When a young father lost his job, a local church (where this father was not a member) heard the story and made the family's mortgage payment for three months.
- On a personal note, I recently connected with Mike Brechtel, a contact from Chalmette, Louisiana, who I knew when he was an eight-year-old at a summer football camp sponsored by my high school football coach. On Facebook, he messaged me that I was his favorite coach (he calls me "Coach Pitch") and thanked me for making camp so much fun. He later sent a gift to me at home. The package contained a Chalmette High coaching shirt. The feeling was overwhelming to open a package from a young man I hardly knew who was thanking me for making a difference in his life as a child. As I read the card, my wife, Sheri, commented on how emotional I had become about this shirt. All I can say is, "Wow!" Acts of lagniappe are simply amazing!

Lagniappe is happening all around you every single day. Many people don't know exactly what it's called, but they do know what it feels like to experience this gift of generosity and caring. How will you begin to show lagniappe on a daily basis?

Lagniappe for leaders is doing the little things that others don't do. What will you do?

Seven eLements of Leadership

Take Action

What will you do to display lagniappe to your family or coworkers? Write it down!

Family _____

_____

_____

_____

Coworkers _____

_____

_____

_____

6

LAUGH LEARN LISTEN LANGUAGE LAGNIAPPE LEGACY LOVE

> *"My mother always told me that as you go through life, no matter what you do, or how you do it, you leave a little footprint, and that's your legacy."*
>
> *Jan Brewer*

Legacy is defined as "something transmitted by or received from an ancestor or predecessor or from the past." Many consider a legacy a gift. In the context of an organization or a team, a legacy is simply leaving a place better than you found it. I'm confident that you have a desire to leave a positive impact on your family, your friends, and your workplace. The question is: will you?

For parents, legacy is evidenced in the lives of family members, and perhaps most importantly, in the lives of children. In the workplace, your legacy is left with your coworkers, those you work with, side by side, year after year. You may leave your legacy in a company by ensuring its financial success or a culture of innovation. Your legacy is indeed the gift you leave with others after you are no longer there.

Death is not a prerequisite for leaving a legacy, as your legacy becomes evident simply by your absence. Every day, successful leaders leave one organization (or department) for their next position, and long after their departure, their legacy lives on. Students and athletes leave their teachers and coaches on an annual basis, and again, a legacy lives on.

What will be your legacy?

Consider this question. Although the answer could appear to be elusive, simply taking time to think through your response will prove productive and enlightening. You will learn that your answer to this question can have an impact on your behavior. If you know how you want to be remembered, you become aware of the actions you must take to create that legacy.

I doubt that my dad thought much about the legacy he would leave his sons. However, his legacy is truly a gift. When my father was fifty-two, he was diagnosed with cancer in his stomach and bladder. He was a seaman and merchant marine, and cancer rendered him unfit for duty. With only a sixth-grade education, his choices for meaningful employment were limited. At times, my father worked three jobs to pay the bills and keep a roof over our heads. At one point, he managed a marina, painted houses on weekends, and opened oysters at a grocery store. The message he continually pounded into my stubborn head: "Stay in school and get a good education."

Every time I complained about schoolwork, his response was emphatic. "Stay in school and get a good education." However, this message was not his legacy. The legacy he left me was the importance of a strong work ethic; whatever your job, do it well. I brought this strong work ethic to every position I have ever held. Many times, that work ethic earned me promotions over men and women who were much more talented and far better educated. Although I never crossed the line of being a workaholic, I generally spent more time doing what needed to be done than most of my peers.

> A legacy is simply leaving a place better than you found it.

So what type of legacy do you want to leave?

This question has no right or wrong answer, but indeed there are many choices. The legacy you leave to your family may be very different from the legacy you leave in your professional life.

A Legacy of Learning. In both your professional and personal life, you could be known as a person who has an insatiable appetite for knowledge. Those who know you well realize you're open to new experiences and that you view each day as a new opportunity to expand your knowledge. Leadership and learning go hand in hand, so this type of legacy serves others extremely well.

A Legacy of Excellence. You are known as someone who constantly pursues excellence in all that you do. In your opinion, good is the archenemy of great, and mediocrity is something you despise. You surround yourself with people who not only want to improve the process, but also improve themselves. A leader who expects excellence is like a rising tide that lifts all boats. By your expectations alone, the performance of the rest of the team begins to improve. You constantly push those around you to bring their "A game" every single day.

A Legacy of Caring. Caring more about others than you care about yourself demonstrates that you lead with your heart. You realize that there are people who are less fortunate and that every day provides you with an opportunity to help those in need. Many people wear the spirit of philanthropy on their heart and enjoy the pleasure of being able to lend a helping hand. At the foundation of this legacy is a knowledge that one person can indeed make a difference. When you truly care about your team, people notice and team members respond. Many leaders have been blessed with financial success that comes with an executive position. Some of these leaders choose to be involved in several philanthropic endeavors and evidence this spirit of caring that impacts many. With this type of leader at the helm, many companies and organizations inject this spirit of caring into their culture.

The legacy I have chosen to leave my family and my coworkers is a legacy of caring. Early in my career, I worked for a few leaders who taught me the valuable lesson of how it feels to work for someone who doesn't give a damn about you as a person. I guess these men and women taught me exactly what not to do. Every situation, good or bad, does indeed provide a learning experience. As a young leader, I decided to create and demonstrate a legacy of caring. Quite to my surprise, that gift of caring was returned to me by my team, allowing me to experience the power of legacy coming full circle.

During my first visit to Sydney to evaluate the future viability of the financing subsidiary, I was given three weeks to do the analysis. It was an extremely difficult decision for me to take this assignment, as my older brother was in Houston at the MD Anderson Cancer Center. He had been diagnosed with multiple myeloma, a terminal type of cancer that in 1994 had a life expectancy after diagnosis of about eighteen months. I had a long discussion with my older brother, one in which he told me that if I stuck around and passed on this opportunity, he would view it as proof that I thought he was going to die soon. While sitting on the end of his hospital bed, we decided that I would make the fourteen-hour flight to Sydney.

On my fourth day in Sydney, I received a call from my sister-in-law that my fifty-one-year-old brother had passed away. By the time I got back to the office, a team of people had already packed my things, gone to the hotel to retrieve my luggage, booked me on the next flight, and prepared to drive me to the Sydney airport. My boss, Mary Maarbjerg, handled a great deal of my itinerary, and she had left me an email with the travel arrangements. "Pitch, take as much time as you need, and call me after your brother's services to talk about next steps," she said on my voicemail. On one of the toughest days of my life, I will never forget the feelings I experienced knowing how these people cared for me. I strive on a daily basis to ensure that the people I work with know how much I care for them.

A Legacy of Innovation. Perhaps Steve Jobs is best known for this legacy at Apple. Jobs continually pushed those close to him to create products and services that the masses didn't even know they wanted. This drive for creativity and innovation is a legacy left by leaders such as Jobs, Gates, and Musk. Each of these leaders demanded their teams view the world through a different lens, while forcing team members to dream big. New technologies are being developed at a blistering pace, and in many of the firms that are at the forefront of these advances, the legacy of innovation is obvious. Yet, this legacy of innovation is not limited to the technology sector; it can be achieved in any passionate pursuit you have.

Ron Clark, a former "National Teacher of the Year" award recipient, is an example of this. His innovative approach to education has been a role model of success for schools throughout the country. Ron leads a school where students dance and sing throughout the day as a part of the learning process. During my interview process for Leadership Atlanta, I had the opportunity to meet Ron and spend several hours in a classroom at his school. The innovative techniques that he has brought into the educational arena seem to have traditional educators scratching their heads. However, the test scores of his students, combined with graduation rates and college scholarships, have parents giving him high fives. Innovation is not just about technology.

A Legacy of Integrity. Integrity is the act of doing the right thing, whether you'll be recognized for it or not. Integrity is based on the choices you make when no one else is watching. It's the difference between right and wrong that you know in your gut. Trouble is when you think you may not be held accountable for your actions, or that no one will know one way or the other, you have to decide what to do. You always have a choice to act with integrity. You'll either listen to "the bad you" on your one shoulder, telling you to change the numbers because no one will know, or you'll listen to "the good you" and report the loss, then make a plan to improve next time.

A Legacy of Hard Work. This is a legacy that can be found in sports teams after a beloved coach retires or moves on to another organization. In a sales organization, hard work often takes the form

Legacy

of one more call at the end of a long day. On the athletic field, hard work is evidenced by the athletes who show up early, train at 100 percent, and stay late. In the classroom, hard work is evidenced by students who go beyond simply reading the text to fully researching the subject.

I have spoken to many colleagues who have not once considered the type of legacy they will leave. For too many people, the question seems foreign, or even silly, to consider. After a guest lecture at Emory University, one MBA candidate explained, "I won't leave a legacy. I'll just leave the job." I asked her to reconsider what type of legacy she wants to leave and to work toward a positive one. If not, the legacy she leaves won't be one she is proud of.

All leaders leave some type of legacy, whether they choose to or not. In your personal life, your legacy is the example you set for your partner and your children. In the business arena, that legacy is left to those you spend countless hours with in the pursuit of success. In education and research, the legacy you leave can touch the lives of thousands or millions, and you may never know the impact or the size of your sphere of influence.

Can you predict what future impact your children could have on the world if you give them a legacy of caring or philanthropy? Could you forecast the potential of your team if your legacy is that of innovation? Think about the possibilities.

A Legacy of Developing People. Many leadership experts comment that this is a leader's most important objective: the development of people. Leaders in almost every organization are tasked with developing the people on their team. Coaches at every level of athletics willingly accept the responsibility for teaching the skills that take their athletes to the next level. In the business arena, coaching and mentoring aspiring talent is a necessity for start-ups and mature organizations alike.

Both the aspiring young leader and the seasoned executive should understand the importance of (and the difference between) two activities: coaching and mentoring. If you want to create a legacy of developing people, become a coach and a mentor.

Coaching doesn't get the respect it deserves, but it's a competency all leaders should master. As a leader, you will be required to coach your team members. Unfortunately, many use the terms coaching and mentoring as interchangeable. They are not. Coaching is teaching a specific set of skills required for success in a specific situation. Mentoring is sharing wisdom so that the mentee has the opportunity to learn from the life experiences of the mentor.

Many sports fans would argue that Jerry Rice was the greatest wide receiver to play in the National Football League. If a rookie in the NFL was blessed to have Jerry Rice teach him the techniques of running a proper pass route or how to concentrate on "looking" the football into his hands, that young man would be blessed to have Rice as his coach. However, if that same young NFL rookie got to spend time with him as Rice explained the virtues of hard work and preparation and discussed the importance of being a positive role model on and off the football field, the young man's blessings would be immensely multiplied by having Rice as his mentor. To simplify, a coach works on specific skills to achieve a task, while a mentor shares wisdom gained through the mentor's life experiences.

On any given day, there is a sales manager who's working with a new sales representative to teach prospecting and cold calling. The sales manager might go in to great detail about how to determine a need that can be met by the product or service the company sells. This type of coaching is invaluable to all who pursue a career in sales. However, something that occurs much less frequently is the young sales professional who meets with a mentor to understand the importance of a strong work ethic, the impact that empathy has in the sales process, or why little things like sending personal notes (lagniappe) create a referral base that can generate additional income.

A coach teaches skills. A mentor shares wisdom. Each role, that of mentor and that of coach, is critical in the development of the student, the athlete, or the business professional. Even if you don't view yourself as a full-fledged coach, look within to identify your coaching skills. These skills could include your ability to provide meaningful feedback, your technical insight, or your time management skills. Accept the role of a coach, and teach others the skills required for success.

Many organizations have defined success in a certain role as mastering specific job competencies. Coaching is an excellent way to teach these competencies. As a leader, your role is to identify the skills required for a particular task, assess your team members' abilities related to a specific skillset, and develop a plan for improvement in each competency.

Early in my career, I received a great deal of coaching on how to coach. In my twenties, I had the opportunity to lead a sales team that struggled to meet objectives for many years. I was very good at closing a sale, so I informed my team that I was available to intercede during the closing stage. Our team began to hit sales objectives on a regular basis, and as anyone in the sales profession knows, when you are successful one year, the objectives get bigger the next year.

The following year, in an effort to maintain our level of success,

I was required to be in additional closing meetings, and when our sales team grew, you guessed it, the demands on my time increased. The pace became unsustainable, and our performance suffered. Instead of teaching my team the steps of the sales process, I had decided it was better to shortcut the process. I wasn't coaching them on the skills necessary to do the job successfully, but rather I was showing off my proficiency in the area of "closing the deal."

Jerry Graham, a dear friend, coached me through this period in my life. He taught me that the ability to coach a team is a fundamental component of building a successful team. Jerry proved to me that showing my team how to successfully navigate the entire sales process would help them be more successful—without my participation on each closing call. I began coaching my team instead of doing the job for them. Fish for a man and you will feed him for a day, but teach a man to fish and he will eat for a lifetime.

Although the subject of coaching is quite broad, there are fundamental elements of coaching that every leader should know:

- **Use conversations as a coaching opportunity.** This is important, as you will begin to use your time wisely. Lunch or breakfast conversations become an opportunity for short coaching sessions. Each day provides countless opportunities to use quick interactions as learning experiences.
- **Be specific.** Accurately describe the specific skills you want your team member to improve. Don't assume your team member knows what skills he or she needs to develop.
- **Set goals.** Create a development plan that includes goals and objectives for the skill or competency you are coaching your team members in.

- **Communicate regularly.** Communicate progress often and discuss any obstacles to success. Your communication is the constructive feedback necessary for successful development. Feedback should include praise and areas of needed improvement so the individual understands when progress is made and when additional work must be done.
- **Share your expectations early.** Articulate your expectations early in the process. Your expectations can be around frequency of sessions, timely feedback, assignments, and results.
- **Model the way.** If the skill or competency you're teaching is something you do very well, remember that you are a role model. Let your team members witness your talent. If you're not the most effective at the skill you're teaching, demonstrate a passionate willingness to learn and improve so your team members see you as an example.
- **Do it.** Learning involves doing, so don't simply tell your team members what to do; show them how it's done, and then let them do it themselves. Let growth naturally flourish by allowing your team members to think through the process and determine the answers on their own. Express that you understand mistakes could happen, and that failure, although not ideal, is an opportunity to learn.
- **Celebrate achievement.** Celebrate the successes. Acknowledgment, recognition, and rewards will motivate your team members to further improve.

Be a coach, find a coach

Serious leaders know that finding a coach is a priority. They also know that choosing the right coach is critical. For many leaders in business, the coaching role is fulfilled by their boss, but it doesn't always have to be so. A coworker or peer can serve as a great coach, as can a human resources specialist, pastor, neighbor, or spouse.

Throughout your leadership journey, you may find several different coaches who are willing to educate you in various areas of development. For example, you may find that a family member could serve as an excellent public speaking coach, while a coworker might coach you on mastering the technology to manage customer interactions. If you have a true thirst for knowledge and personal development, you will find many qualified coaches who are excited to share their skillsets.

To be successful when being coached, you have to be humble. The reality is that you're looking for assistance in developing a skill, most likely one you're not good at. Even the most successful, highly paid leaders use the wisdom and instruction of a coach. Why should you be any different?

Be a mentor, find a mentor

Mentoring is a partnership between two individuals who focus on the personal development of the junior partner. Oftentimes, a mentor will draw on personal experience when mentoring a protégé on personal attributes such as character, integrity, and leadership styles.

The opportunity to serve as a mentor depends on where you are in your own development. Regardless of your tenure in leadership, a healthy dose of confidence mixed with humility, plus the desire to serve others, is the foundation of being a great mentor. Many leaders I speak with feel that they are too new in their leadership journey to serve in a mentoring capacity, but most times they're wrong. Even the first-year manager, perhaps at age twenty-four or twenty-five, has something to offer the college senior who is pursuing a degree in business. A relationship built on trust and mutual respect could be incredibly beneficial to a college student who has yet to experience the pressures of a job interview or the first day on the job. An aspiring leader can serve as a mentor to someone who will soon walk in his or her footsteps.

In her bestselling book, *Lean In*, Facebook Chief Operating Officer Sheryl Sandberg recommends mentoring for women in the business arena. Sandberg says that the strongest relationships spring out of a real connection that is felt by both sides. She goes on to say that there is benefit to both the mentor and the mentee, and when it's done right, everybody flourishes.[13]

Mentoring offers leaders an opportunity to give back. The corporate world has embraced formal mentoring programs, assigning individuals to mentors within their own organizations. Similarly, mentors and mentees can be matched by third parties, such as when the mentor and the mentee are from different companies.

Outside of the corporate arena, being a mentor can take a myriad of paths. You might be asked by a civic organization, such as the Boys and Girls Club, to mentor a teenager you've never met. That might make you a bit nervous, but remember that mentorship is about serving others and giving back. When done correctly, you will revel in the experience of witnessing the "lights going on" for your mentee.

In most cases, the mentee is responsible for driving the men-

---

13 Sheryl Sandberg, Lean In: Women, Work, and the Will to Lead (New York: Knopf Publishing, 2013).

toring relationship. This means that the mentee must do a self-assessment of his or her needs, expectations, topics to discuss, and personal development opportunities. Similarly, as a mentor, you must assess your own readiness and willingness to serve in this important capacity. As the mentor, you will have to build trust, establish effective communication methods, and lead if the relationship gets off track. Effectively managing these roles establishes you as a true leader, one committed to leaving a legacy of caring and developing people.

Can you choose only one legacy?

Yes, you can choose only one legacy, and you must forego any others!

Of course, I'm kidding. While in my heart I want people to remember me as a person who truly cared about people, I'd also like them to remember the success that our teams have achieved. As a leader, you will have the opportunity to influence people in several ways. I do feel, however, that there are one or two dominant themes in your leadership style that will become evident over time. Think about the great leaders who have influenced your life. When you think of them in terms of what legacy these leaders have left, you will immediately think of one or two attributes.

For a teacher, it could be the joy and fun of learning, while you also remember she emphasized hard work. In the business world, you might remember leaders who inspired you to develop your own skills and possibly to take chances. Within your family, you recall relatives who are the caretakers and have developed the legacy of caring for your family. And of course, most of us have memories of our "crazy uncle" who put fun ahead of everything else. By the way, a fun legacy from a family member is something we can all enjoy.

Write your legacy

The point of creating a legacy is that you leave a bit of yourself for others to emulate. One way to share your legacy with others is to write it. This could be in whatever form you feel most comfortable. For me, that written legacy is in the form of the book you're reading.

I began this book project more than a decade ago. After several starts and stops, and with many notebooks and computer files full of unorganized text, I was no closer to a finished book than when I initially had the idea to write it. Thankfully, I met a woman named Anita Henderson, who started a company called Write Your Life. Anita is my writing coach! I really needed a writing coach, as procrastination is one of my personal vices. Anita helps authors write about what they know best. In other words, write about your own life.

When I started this book project, I believed I would be satisfied if I simply produced four copies and gave one to each of my daughters. That would be success for me. I have not changed my position. This book is part of my legacy. The Seven eLements are what I want my daughters, my grandchildren, and others to remember about me. If any of the eLements come to the minds of my family, friends, or coworkers when they think of me now or in the future, I will have enjoyed great success.

So write your legacy. Put ink to paper (or type on your computer) and express what you want your personal or business legacy to be. Give the topic some serious thought. It doesn't have to be more than a paragraph or two. Remember, this is personal. It's yours.

Then take some time of reflection to evaluate whether or not your behavior matches your desire. If you died today (or were abducted by aliens, much less macabre), would your true legacy resemble the legacy you've written? If you give thought each day to your legacy, you will begin to modify your behavior, your beliefs, and your values.

Write your legacy.

Take Action

What will your legacy be? Write it down.

My legacy will be _____

_____

_____

_____

_____

_____

7

"The greatest happiness of life is the conviction that we are loved; loved for ourselves, or rather, loved in spite of ourselves."

Victor Hugo

When I give my leadership presentation in the corporate world, this particular eLement seems to cause the most discomfort. I get to watch the body language of some of the men in the audience change as the slide at the front of the room transitions to four big letters: **L-O-V-E.**

A few members of the audience have posed the question, "Isn't love in the workplace an HR violation?" You have to admit that this response shows a healthy sense of humor.

For many, love is a tough sell in the corporate world. Collectively, people just don't have that much experience understanding this emotion and neatly harnessing its power in the workplace. Although this isn't an easy subject to grasp in the context of a leadership book, if you will read this chapter with an open mind, I am confident that you'll have a new awareness of how this powerful emotion can impact your career and your relationships.

One common currency: Time

I'd like you to do a math problem with me. You will begin with the number 168. This represents the number of hours in a week. To reach the answer to this problem, subtract the amount of time you spend each week doing a certain activity, working toward a last number that I will explain upon completion.

Total hours in a week	168
Less Hours spent sleeping (if you sleep 8 hours a night x 7 = 56)	XX
Less Hours spent commuting to work	XX
Less Hours spent on hygiene (shower, make-up, getting ready for work)	XX
Less Hours spent exercising	XX
Less Hours spent learning / reading	XX
Less Number of hours at WORK (example, 9 hrs./day, 5 days/week = 45)	XX
What's left?	???

As this is something that I've calculated on a regular basis, I'd like to share my results with you.

Total hours in a week	168
Less Hours spent sleeping	56
(I need 8 hours x 7; what can I say?)	
Less Hours spent commuting to work	5
Less Hours spent on hygiene	6
(shower, make-up, getting ready for work)	
Less Hours spent exercising	6
(This needs to be more, I know.)	
Less Hours spent learning / reading	6
Less Number of hours at WORK	48
What's left?	41

What's left

Think about the numbers in this equation. These numbers represent your life. The work entry is listed at the very end of the equation for a reason—to highlight how much time many people spend at their vocation. For many, work is a passion, a calling, or perhaps it's just a job. Regardless of what emotion you attach to your livelihood, the point is that most people spend as many waking hours working as they do with those they love (family and friends). If your final number is anything similar to that of the majority of people in the world, you might as well do something you love. It has been said, "Do something you love, and you will never work another day in your life."

The "what's left" is your *life*, the time you spend with your loved ones enjoying the fruits of all the labor you've invested in the other numbers. The "what's left" are hours for date nights, sporting events, the kids' soccer games, and trips to the beach. The hours left are the walks with your partner, the early morning coffee with your mom or dad, and the times spent with your children. The hours left are the most meaningful times in your life and the hours that create the memories you will reflect on in your winter years. In very simple terms, this is what gives life meaning.

Many people who do this exercise are amazed by the last two sets of numbers, representing the amount of hours spent at work and the number of hours remaining to spend with family and friends. For many, the two numbers are very close. I would wager that for many young men and women who are early in their careers, much more time is spent building a career than living life. I also would suggest that this result is a personal choice. I have spoken to young attorneys and financial professionals who said, "Anything less than a hundred-hour work week will get me fired." That is a personal choice. As is the choice of members of a younger generation who want to spend more time on altruistic endeavors than in personal career advancement. Again, this is a personal choice.

The significance of what's left changes as you age. The speed at which each of these hours passes accelerates rapidly. I guess I'm a "chronologically gifted" executive (not politically correct to say "old"), who is simply advising you to stop and smell the roses. However, that subject is for a book to be written on another day.

Love in the workplace?

When the subject of love in the workplace is raised, many people immediately think of love in the romantic context. Professor Olivia O'Neill, of George Mason University, introduces a different perspective in her research titled "Does Love Belong in the Workplace?" Here is O'Neill's description of what she calls "companionate love."

> "Companionate love takes place in the relationships that form the majority of our interactions. It involves affection, caring and compassion and has a much broader scope than romantic love—it can be experienced in the workplace, friendships and family relationships. In strong cultures of love, we observe that people care about one another's well-being; they look out for one another and pick up the slack for one another. A culture of love is not just something that takes place between two people, rather something that is pervasive throughout the organization."[14]

Think about the work or team experiences that you have enjoyed the most. The environment was probably one that fostered a feeling of caring and was a place where people had your back. O'Neill says that a culture of love is not just for couples, but for companies. I am convinced that this kind of corporate culture creates a competitive advantage. It is also one of the most difficult cultures to build because it starts at the top. This type of culture starts with a leader who understands the importance of servant leadership and the idea that he or she is there to serve the interests of others.

When members of an organization genuinely sense this feeling of service from their leadership, the behavior becomes pervasive. When a leader begins to show appreciation, listen to suggestions, and put his or her needs after the needs of the team, these behaviors become common practice. The team reflects the behavior of its leadership. What culture is your leadership creating? If you're uncertain, ask people you trust. They will tell you.

---

14 Olivia O'Neill and Sigal G. Barade, "What's Love Got to Do with It," Administrative Science Quarterly (May 29, 2014): 4.

Seven eLements of Leadership

Love creates enthusiasm

"Enthusiasm is one of the most powerful engines of success. When you do a thing, do it with all your might. Put your whole soul into it. Stamp it with your own personality. Be active, be energetic, be enthusiastic and faithful, and you will accomplish your objective. Nothing great was ever achieved without enthusiasm."
Ralph Waldo Emerson

As you think about outstanding leaders in your own life, you will recall that many of them were brimming with enthusiasm. From corporate boardrooms, to the classroom, to athletic fields across this great nation, enthusiastic leaders can often be found leading a group of enthusiastic supporters. It is the conviction of these leaders that stirs the conviction in those they lead. Great leaders don't have followers; they have supporters who make a choice to support the chosen cause, course of action, or desired outcome. Remember that great leaders influence always, and they always do so with enthusiasm.

When you love your chosen field, your enthusiasm tends to be infectious. Those around you begin to use the words, the tone, and perhaps even the body language of you, their leader. When you truly love what you do, that love creates enthusiasm. Each day you make a choice of how you will live that day. From walking into your first class, to walking into your place of employment, to sitting in church, you and only you choose how you will face the day. Enthusiasm is a choice. Facing the day with joy and excitement is a choice. As a leader, others will follow your lead. Why? Because as a leader, you influence always.

If you are married, this choice starts even earlier in the morning when you wake up next to your partner. Even for those who admit to not being "a morning person," a smile and a kiss is a great way to start a morning. When you wake, realize you have been blessed with another day and what you make of that gift is up to you. Choose wisely.

I often ask people to think about their very first day in their current position and use one word to describe their emotions. The most popular words are "excited" and "enthusiastic." I then ask them, "What about now?" Rarely do they use either word. What happened? What's the difference? Time and familiarity can take a toll on your level of enthusiasm, but you are responsible for this emotion. Find something in your role or your vocation that excites you and lock into that opportunity. What about your role gives you satisfaction? If you continue to wake up for months or years without being able to answer that question, it's time to start looking for something else to do.

Love solidifies commitment

There is a fable about commitment. The short version involves two farm animals—a chicken and a pig—discussing a possible business relationship to open a new breakfast restaurant called Ham and Eggs. After a few moments of listening to the chicken's bounding enthusiasm about the business opportunity, the pig wisely declines the offer, explaining to the chicken, "In this arrangement, I would be totally committed, and you would only be involved." The humor in the fable is that the pig has to give his all to this partnership, while the chicken offers much less of a commitment to its success.

On several occasions, I have spoken with young men and women in the military about their service, and the phrase "love of country" is often used. Many in law enforcement use similar statements about protecting the communities where they live and work. It's obvious that these individuals did not choose their profession for fame or fortune. Men and women serving in these vocations should have our respect and our admiration for the roles they fill in protecting us and those we love.

Love solidifies your commitment to your family members, to your friends, to your local community, to your country, and yes, even to your company. Commitment to an athletic team means devoting long hours of practice. In the business world, commitment can be demonstrated by making the last sales call or follow-up call of the day before heading home. The desired commitment could take the form of countless hours of software development, checking the Excel spreadsheet for the one hundredth time, or even staying after class to help the sophomore who's struggling to solve the algebra equation. You can easily identify the committed members of your team by the behaviors they demonstrate.

Years ago, as a young sales director with Pitney Bowes, I had the opportunity to work with a vice president named Rick Butzek. Rick was a caring and gregarious leader from Chicago. In a fourth-quarter push for sales, our region was in competition for "Region of the Year" recognition against three other contenders in the company. Success meant working right up to New Year's Eve. At that time, the revenue from a sale could not be recognized unless the office equipment was delivered to the customer's address. Many of us gave up holiday time to ensure that we could recognize enough leased business to win "Region of the Year" honors. My colleagues and I didn't do this for ourselves. We didn't do this because Rick asked us to (which he did not). We committed to do this for Rick. We wanted him to have that recognition. When the team was working until 10 o'clock at night, Rick was in the office with everyone else. People are committed to a person or a cause, not a company or an organization. Do your team members show this level of commitment? Does your leadership style warrant this type of commitment?

Love ignites passion

Passion has become a vogue term in the business world. I have concerns that it's becoming a corporate buzzword that no one really understands, sort of like synergy. The four core values of LeasePlan are Passion, Expertise, Respect, and Commitment. When our company was debating the selection of the values that we aspired to, I was extremely passionate about the word "passion." In the end, I agreed with the values chosen, and I took the position that passion does not just happen.

As a company, we hire passionate people, but we have to create an environment where this passion can thrive. Today, we have created a company environment where team members who are passionate about sports can play flag football, softball, or join a bowling league. Those of us who are passionate about helping others can join a group called LeasePlan Cares, which is responsible for our philanthropic efforts. We support Weight Watchers programs and running groups for those who are passionate about their health and fitness. We have maintained these values over the course of the last several years, and as an organization, we believe they're more than pretty posters on our walls. When asked how we've created this kind of culture, I respond that we hire passionate people, and then we give them the opportunity to express their passion in creative ways that foster employee engagement and employee satisfaction.

Love is the flame that ignites passion. You can immediately determine when someone is passionate about their work or profession by the way they talk about it. Most likely you've been at a party or family gathering and had a conversation with someone who loves their work. Their body language, tone, and words all indicate that they truly love what they do. It's obvious, and sometimes, it is enviable.

Passion can't be faked; you're either passionate about something or you're not. If you think you can become more passionate about your work or your life by reading this book, think again! No one and no book can ignite passion for you. Take a look in the mirror and realize that the person looking back is the only one who can determine what you're passionate about. You won't find passion in your work until you find work you love doing. What do you love to do? Where is your passion?

You are the only person who can truly answer these two questions.

Love and engagement

In 1964, the Righteous Brothers hit the top of the charts, in both the U.S. and the U.K., with a song titled "You've Lost That Lovin' Feeling." I'm fairly confident that the Righteous Brothers had no idea that fifty years later, their pop hit could be considered an anthem for the average worker.

Sadly, many use the word "hate" to describe how they feel about their current vocation. Today, the term "employee engagement," rather than "employee satisfaction," is being used to determine high performance organizations. In Gallup's 2013 "State of the American Workplace" study, an alarming 70 percent of Americans reported they either hated their jobs or they were completely disengaged. The survey, which polled 150,000 full- and part-time workers, indicated that only about 30 percent honestly enjoyed what they did for a living. Why do you think seven out of ten people responded this way to a completely anonymous survey?

Jim Clifton, CEO of Gallup, the world's largest polling organization, stated that poor management is one of the leading causes for employee disengagement. With all due respect to Mr. Clifton, I disagree. I am confident that at the core of such pathetic results on employee engagement is poor *leadership*. The engagement of employees in an organization is greatly impacted by the tone at the top. The employee-supervisor relationship is a two-way dynamic, and the employee is equally responsible for his or her engagement. Leadership begins with you, and if you can't lead and influence yourself, why would anyone ever want to support and follow you?

Every day, people wake up and go to work. Not everyone can be working on a cure for cancer, fighting for justice for the average Joe in front of a jury, or creating the next social media Internet darling. However, everyone can find meaning in their work. You determine what you are passionate about. You owe it to yourself (and your family) to find that passion in your work. You are responsible for finding an engaging career that gets you out of bed in the morning. I've been told by HR professionals at LeasePlan that I shouldn't be telling new hires that if they aren't happy at the company in six months, they should quit. I continue to ignore my HR colleagues because I'm confident that this is sage advice. Only you, as the employee and future leader, can make this call. I strongly suggest that if you don't like where you work after six months, you probably won't be *more* satisfied in six years.

Before there is a rush to exit the corporate world, allow me to make a suggestion. Is it possible to get that "day one" feeling back? I believe it is indeed possible to reignite the flame, but first you must answer some tough questions.

1. What attributes of your work do you truly enjoy?
2. Is there something about your current job that you could find passion in?
3. What could spark a new level of enthusiasm or engagement?
4. How can you make a new commitment to your work?

It's important that, after you review these questions, you begin to take action. I advise my team members to answer these questions and write down the three things they love about where they work and the work they do. It's therapeutic to see on paper what you love about your work.

You, like most leaders, will go through a tough patch in your career. No one would suggest that, after a couple months of long work weeks or a dry spell in sales, you should tell the boss to take this job and shove it. However, for the most part, you will know when that tough patch has turned into the "valley of death."

My son-in-law, Ryan, has been in a management training program for Chick-fil-A for the past three years. He worked his way through college while at the University of Georgia, and after graduation, he began working sixty-hour weeks as a manager at the Chick-fil-A store in Athens, Georgia. The Chick-fil-A business model is very different from a standard franchise organization, and it allows young men and women the opportunity to become an operator of up to two locations—without having to invest hundreds of thousands of dollars to start, as one would with the typical fast food franchise.

At the beginning of his career, I recall thinking, *Why would someone go to college for four years and work sixty-hour weeks to sell chicken sandwiches?* I should also explain that this young man proposed to and married my daughter between their sophomore and junior years at UGA, so I had a very suspicious eye on Mr. Ryan Roberts. Knowing that a corporate interview would eventually take place, my son-in-law asked for my assistance in perfecting his interview skills. I know a popular question in many interviews is "Why do you want this job?" So as Ryan and I sat down, I asked, "Why do you want this job, and why Chick-fil-A?" His eyes lit up as he answered the question and spoke about the ability to make a difference in people's lives. His mission was to hire high school and college students and provide them with a way to pay for their education, while teaching them about leadership and management.

He addressed the customer service piece of creating a unique experience for the customers that would come to his store. He passionately talked about becoming an important part of the community he would eventually join by working with elementary schools and high schools on fundraising activities. He wanted to be part of an organization that has provided millions of dollars in scholarships to college students who need financial assistance.

I recall my embarrassment at viewing his role as "just selling chicken sandwiches." Clearly, my son-in-law had an enthusiasm, commitment, passion, and engagement for what he believed this company could do in the community. In a word, he *loves* what this company stands for. I now have a new perspective on the profound impact that local business owners have on their employees and their communities. One could certainly argue that there are franchise and fast food operators who could care less about developing leaders and creating stronger communities; however, that didn't stop one young man from being one who does. His engagement in his own career, and in the company he chose to work for, has made a profound impact on his life. We continue to enjoy mutually beneficial conversations about developing people, honing effective communication skills, and being a servant leader.

Success: My dad's definition

Much of what you learn in life comes from the experiences you share with family, friends, and colleagues. The experiences create phenomenal learning opportunities as you begin to discuss your feelings. Sharing many meaningful experiences with my dad has had a profound impact on the person I am today. The way I live and my view of success are both directly tied to the influence of my dad.

After my father had lived with me for more than eighteen months, he asked me to take him for a couple of beers so we could have a man-to-man talk. At this time, Dad was in a later part of Stage 2 Alzheimer's. He was functional on a daily basis; he still knew his wife and children, but had begun to forget his grandchildren's names, and his short-term memory was deteriorating rapidly. I thought it odd for him to want to go outside of our home for this talk, but I agreed.

We reached our local watering hole and placed our order, and I smiled when he said how much he loved going to new bars with me.

"I need to go to a nursing home in New Orleans," my dad blurted out.

> **Success is empty without love: the love of family, the enthusiasm for work, the commitment to others' success, and a burning passion for life.**

"What are you talking about, Pop?" I asked. I didn't understand where this could be coming from. "I thought you loved being around the girls, watching football with me, and having your own room in the house."

"Well, Michael, let me tell you why." Then he took a long sip of his Budweiser (regular Bud, not the light stuff everyone drinks these days). With cloudy blue eyes that were once clear and steel blue, he said, "Every day when you walk through the door, your wife wants your time, the girls want your time, and then I want your time. There only needs to be one man of the house, and you have only so much time to give your family."

I was stunned. My dad spoke with such clarity and conviction. Obviously, he had given this decision a lot of thought, and I knew I couldn't talk him out of it, although I hoped that if I waited it out, he might forget about it altogether and be happy living with us in Atlanta. That didn't happen.

Each morning he would ask me about the progress on finding him a new place in New Orleans. My older brother and I did the research and found a brand new adult nursing home directly across the street from a hospital in Chalmette, Louisiana. This facility was less than three miles from the home we were raised in, the home that my parents owned for fifty years. After completing all the required paperwork, the only thing left was for my dad to move into his new residence. We had some of his personal items shipped to his new home, and I decided to load up my car and make the seven-hour drive from Atlanta to New Orleans with my dad to get a feeling for his attitude about this move. I wanted to make sure that the move back to New Orleans was something he wanted to do.

Since our old home was now vacant and still contained the rest of my dad's things, we could arrive at any time we wanted. So we decided to take a leisurely drive to the Crescent City on a Sunday to avoid the traffic headaches. Two hours into the drive, my dad seemed agitated. He started picking at his face and scratching his neck. Something was wrong with Pops, and I was convinced it was the thought of moving into the nursing home. I questioned him about it, and his response was the same each time. "I'm fine. Just drive."

When we crossed the Mississippi border, I asked if he wanted to stop for a beer.

"Pull over at the next exit, I'm buying!" was his enthusiastic response.

After a couple of beers, he confessed that he was really worried about some of the things in the old house. He explained that he was concerned about some valuable things he left behind in the New Orleans home when he moved to Atlanta, and he wanted to make sure they were safe. When I was a kid, we lived in an 800-square-foot home and my dad worked three jobs to put his three sons through college. One of my dad's proudest moments was paying off his bank loan and burning the mortgage paperwork at a party. So I thought his most valuable possession was his home, not something that was in his house. I reassured him that we would stop at the house and get him anything he wanted for his new place.

"Let's roll," was his response after his cold beer.

At the Louisiana border, his agitation got worse. He started picking at his cheek and his ear, and I noticed a small drop of blood dripping down the side of his face.

"Pops, what the matter? I'm really worried about you. If you don't want to go to this nursing home, I can turn the car around and head back to Atlanta."

His response came quickly. "Just get us home so I can get to my room. I just need to get to my room." His behavior was very confusing and irrational.

Finally, we arrived in the neighborhood where I grew up in New Orleans. This was prior to Hurricane Katrina, which devastated the area in 2005. After that disaster, our family home would be under water for twenty-seven days and eventually fall over in pieces when a crane tapped the side of the house with a wrecking ball. As we got closer to the house, I watched my dad's physical appearance change. He stopped picking at his face, he sat straight up, and he carefully assessed his surroundings.

"The Prices painted their shutters green. Ugly shade of green if you ask me," he quipped.

My car hadn't come to a complete stop in our family's driveway yet, when he opened the door to jump out. My eighty-two-year-old father literally opened the door to jump out of the car!

"Pops, take it easy. We'll get your stuff," I said to reassure him.

The reassurance made no difference in his behavior. He trotted up the walkway and up the three-step porch. I had called the movers ahead of time, so the front door was already unlocked. Pops turned the handle, opened the door, and ran inside. I was literally running behind him. He went through the living room, then the small kitchen, and then he turned into the family room and dashed to the back of the house where his bedroom was located.

I stopped in the kitchen and remembered having breakfast at the bar with two stools. I noticed the stand-alone stove, the knotty pine walls, the single sink, and the air conditioning unit in the window. My home in Atlanta had a finished basement the size of this entire house. I remember thinking that my car cost more than this house. Lost in those memories and thoughts of my success, the sounds of my dad rummaging through a closet brought me back to the present and our reason for being there. A wave of guilt poured over me like an August rain in New Orleans.

I saw my dad walk through the door with a cigar box and a leather bomber jacket. He was cool and calm. "Michael, before we go to the new place, can we stop and get a six-pack? I don't really know the rules, but I hope they'll let me have a couple of cold ones every now and then."

I was shocked. What the hell just happened? A cigar box and a leather jacket was all he wanted to get from the house.

"Dad, what's in the box?"

"Couple of things, no big deal," he said, then his signature line, "Let's roll."

"Dad, what's in the box?" I asked, as my curiosity grew.

"Maybe a twelve-pack would be better," he said with a smile, "and maybe we can get the tall boys!"

As he stood in front of me completely relaxed and smiling, I was ready to throw my five-foot-seven-inch, eighty-two-year-old father to the ground and fight him for the contents of that box. What was so damn important in that little cigar box?

"Dad, c'mon, what's in the box?"

With his eyes a much clearer blue, he opened the cigar box, and to my surprise, I saw postcards from my brother Robbie when he lived in Greece. There were letters from me, sent when I lived in Australia. The contents included Cub Scout pins and newspaper clippings about my brother Danny's band from college. The box was full of memorabilia from his three sons.

Love

"Michael, I needed this box. This is how I know that I was successful. My three sons told me that they were proud of me, that they loved me. I am a very successful man."

My father never finished the sixth grade. During the Depression, he worked multiple jobs, which sometimes required twelve hours each day, to support his family, so he had to quit school. I value my dad's definition of success. I hope someday to be as successful as he was. That day, I learned that success is empty without love: the love of family, the enthusiasm for work, the commitment to others' success, and a burning passion for life.

My father passed away in 2001 at eighty-four years of age. I often think about the events of that day and the contents of that cigar box. He knew he was successful because his children loved him. I still prefer his definition of success over any other I've heard.

Take Action

As a leader, love is shown through your passion and engagement. What three things can you do to display love in your workplace?

1. _____
2. _____
3. _____

Here's a Lagniappe challenge (a little something extra). What three things can you do to display how much you love your family?

1. _____
2. _____
3. _____

Epilogue: My Wish

My wish, first and foremost, is that you realize that you are indeed a leader. If you will accept my definition, you will agree that, at some point, we all carry the mantle of leadership.

Leadership = Influence

In a marriage, you have a great deal of influence with your spouse or partner. As a member of your church, you influence other members of the congregation. As an officer in a college fraternity or sorority, you influence other members on a regular basis. This is leadership. If you are passionate about philanthropic work, when you show up as a volunteer, you are influencing the behavior of others, so this activity is indeed another example of leadership. Of course, the obvious roles of politician or business executive place you firmly in a leadership position.

My wish is that you realize that leadership opportunities are all around you. Leadership is not the private domain of politicians and corporate executives. In fact, many in those positions have provided fine examples of what *not* to do in a leadership capacity.

My wish is that you realize that everyone has an important sphere of influence. Within your sphere of influence are your coworkers, your family, your friends, and maybe even those who follow you on social media. With leadership comes great responsibility. Part of this responsibility should be to reach your full potential as a leader. The first step in this process is to recognize the fact that you are indeed a leader.

I do have a special call-out to the teachers and professors of our schools and universities. I don't think that many consider those in the profession of education as comprising an essential layer of leadership today. This is a fatal mistake. These dedicated men and women, who work for passion, not for pay, will influence the success of future generations. Teachers and professors are owed a profound and sincere debt of gratitude for what they do. In addition, they need support for their efforts on a regular basis, as they attempt to equip students with the skills and knowledge to compete in a global economy.

In the private sector, I speak to many aspiring leaders who underestimate the importance of their role at their company. From new supervisors and managers to senior level directors and vice presidents, many of these leaders-in-training discount the importance of their influence over their teams. The leader sets the tone for the team. This is described as the "tone at the top." Leadership is about influence, and as the leader, you influence always.

> **If you are in a position to influence others, then you are in a leadership role.**

My wish: You influence in the way you say good morning when you walk in the door.

My wish: You influence while having an uplifting conversation about the success of the new software application that the technology team developed.

My wish: You influence when you find yourself sitting in a meeting and looking at your iPhone while a junior executive makes her first presentation and you realize you should put the phone down.

You influence always. Your attitude about change, your attitude about learning, and your attitude about diversity all have an impact on those around you, those in your direct line of supervision and those who are not direct reports.

My wish is that you become aware of the impact that your leadership has on everyone around you.

My wish is that you embrace:

Laugh, Learn, Listen, Language, Lagniappe, Legacy, Love

People want to be inspired. How can you utilize the Seven eLements to create an environment where people are inspired to thrive? The answer is to begin using the Seven eLements in your daily life.

Laugh: Let your team know that you're not a robot. Allow them to see the human side of you and that you're a person who can laugh at a joke, a funny situation, or even at a mistake made by them (or you).

Learn: Have a thirst for knowledge that models this critical behavior of a leader. Be known as the leader who realizes you don't know everything and as the leader who thirsts for new learning.

Listen: Be the leader who understands the desires (and dreams) of others and who listens prior to making decisions. Let people know that their input is important.

Language: Be the inclusive communicator who speaks with passion, purpose, and commitment. Become the storyteller who spreads positive messages and images throughout your organization (and your family).

Lagniappe: Do more than is expected of you as a leader and watch as others do more than you expect of them.

Legacy: Become a teacher and share your knowledge, experience, and wisdom with others by leaving wherever you are a better place than it was when you found it.

Love: Live with passion in your life. Realize that what you do is not who you are and share an attitude of gratitude with those you meet. Be thankful.

Clearly, the Seven eLements are not a shopping list from which to choose what you want now, later, or never. They are ingredients to success that work together, all the time, forever! My wish is that you practice incorporating these elements into your leadership persona, one at a time, and then use the next to build upon the last. Do not strive for perfection; instead strive for progress. And strive to be a complete leader who exemplifies each of the Seven eLements in your leadership journey.

Final thoughts

My final wish is to say thank you for reading this book. You have invested the gift of your time. Regardless of your age, gender, profession, or wealth, you can never get that time back. Time is truly our common currency, and twenty-four hours of a day is exactly what each of us is allotted. I hope you will feel that the time spent reading this book was an investment in your future.

Leadership is not easy. The concept of a born leader is ridiculous. Yes, many are blessed with certain physical traits that could help their career, but successful leadership cannot be maintained by strong cheekbones, a great voice, or a pleasing physical presence. Leadership takes time and energy, and on many days, the effort to master it will exhaust you and drain your spirits. To be blunt, there are days that a path of leadership kicks your ass! (I debated using other words to express this point, but nothing works like the truth.)

The leadership journey has no real end; it is continuous and evolving. If any of the Seven eLements in the leadership journey are discarded, there could be trouble ahead. You could, however, be capable of successfully navigating this journey by using only a few. An exceptional leader in 1990, who since then has allowed his or her skills to go undeveloped, could easily be irrelevant in 2016 and beyond. The world is changing at an incredible pace, and it's being reshaped by the Internet and other factors. There is incredible work to be done for anyone who wants to remain a relevant leader in the future.

There are times when leadership is lonely. Leadership requires making difficult decisions, and there will be times when your decisions are not popular and no one is singing your praises. In those times, my mother used to remind me, "Michael, this too shall pass." I ask you to consider that leadership is one of the most rewarding experiences in life. This is not a statement about money, power, or position. Done with the right attitude and objectives, leadership is a rewarding experience that brings joy and satisfaction to your life and the lives of those you influence. When those who have chosen to support and follow you learn by your example and become leaders in their own right, you will enjoy a feeling of accomplishment that will last the rest of your life.

I have been blessed with the opportunity to work with many amazing people. I've tried to tell so many of them about the positive impact they have had in my life. I've truly loved the relationships that I've shared with so many colleagues over the years. I am blessed to be married to my best friend, my wife, Sheri. Every day, we have the opportunity to laugh, learn, and love together. I deeply love my four daughters, Lauren, Michelle, Mckensie, and Morgan, for the incredible young women they have become. They were amazing children to parent, and now each of them has become an exceptional woman to befriend. There are times when we, as a family, pass the baton of leadership among us. I share these personal reflections to point out that your cloak of leadership is equally important at home as it is elsewhere. In fact, your most important leadership role is that which you enjoy with your family and your friends.

Making a conscious decision to live and enjoy each of the Seven eLements on a regular basis will allow you to look back on your leadership journey years from now and smile, knowing you enjoyed a rich life, not necessarily defined by monetary wealth, but rather a wealth and abundance of amazing relationships and experiences.

Leadership is a journey. Enjoy the ride.

About the Author

Michael "Mike" A. Pitcher is the President and CEO of LeasePlan USA, one of the leading fleet management companies in the United States. Mike has held senior management positions in large multinational firms Pitney Bowes and Dell Computer. He has degrees from the University of Louisiana Lafayette and an MBA from Emory University, in Atlanta.

Mike has been married to his wife, Sheri, since 2007, and their family includes four daughters, Lauren, Michelle, Mckensie, and Morgan. Mike and Sheri have two sons-in-law, Jay and Ryan (married to Lauren and Michelle). The couple also has three grandchildren, Brayden, Riley, and Bella. They are now empty nesters who reside in Alpharetta, Georgia, with two golden retrievers named Lucky and Boudreaux.

Mike is a guest lecturer at Emory University and the University of Georgia. He presents "The Seven eLements of Leadership" to corporate and business gatherings throughout the United States. He also presents "How to Save a Life!" a dynamic presentation on the dangers of distracted driving, and how to have a positive impact on this issue.

To learn more about Mike, or to book him as a speaker, visit www.MikePitcher.net.

Suggested reading for leaders

As We Speak
Peter Meyers and Shann Nix

Attitude Is Everything For Success: Say It, Believe It, Receive it
Keith D. Harrell

First, Break All the Rules: What the World's Greatest Managers Do Differently
Marcus Buckingham

Good to Great: Why Some Companies Make the Leap . . . and Others Don't
Jim Collins

How Full Is Your Bucket?
Tom Rath and Donald Clifton

It Worked For Me: In Life and Leadership
Colin Powell

Joy at Work: A Revolutionary Approach to Fun On the Job
Dennis W. Bakke

Leadership Is an Art
Max DePree

Lean In: Women, Work, and the Will to Lead
Sheryl Sandberg

Love Is the Killer App: How to Win Business and Influence Friends
Tim Sanders

Seven eLements of Leadership

Managing the Generational Mix: From Urgency to Opportunity
Carolyn Martin, PhD and Bruce Tulgan

Now, Discover Your Strengths
Marcus Buckingham, Donald O. Clifton, PhD

Nuts! Southwest Airlines' Crazy Recipe For Business and Personal Success
Kevin Freiberg, Jackie Freiberg

The 21 Irrefutable Laws of Leadership: Follow Them and People Will Follow You
John C. Maxwell

The Five Love Languages: How to Express Heartfelt Commitment to Your Mate
Gary Chapman

The Happiness Advantage
Shawn Achor

The Leader's Voice: How Your Communication Can Inspire Action and Get Results!
Boyd Clarke, Ron Crossland

The Leadership Challenge: How to Make Extraordinary Things Happen in Organizations
James M. Kouzes, Barry Z. Posner

The Seven Habits of Highly Successful People: Powerful Lessons in Personal Change
Stephen R. Covey